Brain-Compatible Differentiated Instruction for English Language Learners

Brain-Compatible Differentiated Instruction for English Language Learners

Marjorie Hall Haley

George Mason University

PEARSON

Boston   New York   San Francisco
Mexico City   Montreal   Toronto   London   Madrid   Munich   Paris
Hong Kong   Singapore   Tokyo   Cape Town   Sydney

Executive Editor: Aurora Martínez Ramos
Series Editorial Assistant: Jacqueline Gillen
Vice President, Marketing and Sales Strategies: Emily Williams Knight
Vice President, Director of Marketing: Quinn Perkson
Executive Marketing Manager: Krista Clark
Production Editor: Annette Joseph
Editorial Production Service: Omegatype Typography, Inc.
Composition Buyer: Linda Cox
Manufacturing Buyer: Megan Cochran
Electronic Composition: Omegatype Typography, Inc.
Interior Design: Omegatype Typography, Inc.
Cover Designer: Elena Sidorova

For Professional Development resources, go to www.allynbaconmerrill.com.

TESOL standards on pages 22–23, 43, 50, 57, 64, 71, 79, and 95 are excerpted from the *Pre-K–12 English Language Proficiency Standards* (2006). Copyright 2006 by Teachers of English to Speakers of Other Languages. Reproduced with permission of Teachers of English to Speakers of Other Languages via Copyright Clearance Center.

Between the time website information is gathered and then published, it is not unusual for some sites to have closed. Also, the transcription of URLs can result in typographical errors. The publisher would appreciate notification where these errors occur.

Library of Congress Cataloging-in-Publication Data

Haley, Marjorie Hall.
   Brain-compatible differentiated instruction for English language learners / Marjorie Hall Haley.
        p.   cm.
   Includes bibliographical references and index.
   ISBN-13: 978-0-205-58239-6 (pbk.)
   ISBN-10: 0-205-58239-7 (pbk.)
   1. English language—Study and teaching—Foreign speakers.   2. Learning, Psychology of.   3. Individualized instruction.   I. Title.
   PE1128.A2H278 2010
   428.2'4—dc22

                                                                                2009003429

Printed in the United States of America

10 9 8 7 6 5 4 3 2 1   14 13 12 11 10 09

www.pearsonhighered.com

ISBN-10: 0-205-58239-7
ISBN-13: 978-0-205-58239-6

About the Author

Marjorie Hall Haley is a tenured professor of education in the Graduate School of Education at George Mason University in Fairfax, Virginia. She is a former Spanish, French, German, and ESL teacher of fourteen years. Dr. Haley holds a Ph.D. in foreign language education and English as a second language from the University of Maryland, College Park. She has also earned a master's degree in education and advanced studies certificates from Towson University and Johns Hopkins University, respectively.

In her twentieth year at George Mason University, she teaches foreign language methods and ESL methods courses as well as doctoral courses in brain-compatible teaching and learning, bilingualism, and second language acquisition research. She is actively involved in ongoing action research projects with teachers at local, national, and international levels. She has conducted four international teacher action research studies focused on the impact of implementing the multiple intelligences theory in foreign and second language classes. These studies included over 3,000 students in fourteen states and six countries. In 2002 George Mason University awarded her its Outstanding Faculty Award in Teaching.

Dr. Haley's research and publication record is wide, including *Content-Based Second Language Teaching and Learning: An Interactive Approach* (2004), book chapters, articles, and scholarly essays. In addition, she is a featured scholar in the WGBH and Annenberg/CPB video "Valuing Diverse Learners," available at www.learner.org.

Contents

Section Two Planning for Brain-Compatible Differentiated Instruction: One-Day Lessons   41

Preface

This book is intended for use by English as a second language (ESL) and mainstream educators—both pre- and in-service teachers. There are five one-day lesson plans and two five-day units, with activities that demonstrate sustained teaching. Each lesson addresses a different topic area and grade level.

Today more than ever, you will encounter diversity in the student population, bringing both challenges and opportunities. The purpose of this book is to prepare teachers to effectively teach brain-compatible differentiated lessons to English language learners (ELLs) while developing students' language ability. The book is intended for teachers of culturally, linguistically, and cognitively diverse learners in K–12 school settings to provide additional resources for teachers to understand how to create brain-compatible differentiated teaching strategies while demonstrating sustained teaching.

What do I mean by *sustained* teaching? As a methods professor I observe my students doing very well with creating and implementing micro teaching simulations. This, in my opinion, is just a snapshot of what teaching should be. Even my student teachers do quite well with this in their school-based assignments. However, when I look for sustained teaching in lessons that continue beyond day one, there is often a void. Additionally, when working with English language learners, the necessity to differentiate instruction is paramount. What I hope to do in this book is to demonstrate for both ESL and mainstream educators who teach through content how to create and sustain teaching throughout a five-day plan of activities while differentiating instruction for culturally, linguistically, and cognitively diverse students using brain-compatible strategies and assessment practices. The activities focus on the TESOL [Teachers of English to Speakers of Other Languages] *ESL Standards for Pre-K–12 Students* and the *Pre-K–12 English Language Proficiency Standards.* Step-by-step activities demonstrate how to address multiple intelligences and different learning styles.

Brain-Compatible Differentiated Instruction for English Language Learners is written for those teachers who are looking for solid instructional practices that work well with mainstream students as well as English language learners. Not intended to be a recipe book for automatic successful teaching, the content provided does not suggest a quick fix. Rather, the intent is to provide you with information necessary to make informed and skillful decisions regarding instructional practices that are likely to be effective in addressing the needs of English language learners.

As an English as a second language methods professor in a graduate school of education, it is incumbent on me to ensure that my students are trained to work with culturally, linguistically, and cognitively diverse students. I assume responsibility to work with pre- and in-service teachers to identify the various kinds of learner diversities, to create a variety of teaching strategies for diverse populations, and to develop a context and framework for differentiating instruction to meet the needs of students in their classrooms. According to Standard and Poor's School Data Direct (n.d.), English language learners (ELLs) comprised 8.5 percent of the nation's K–12 students in 2006. Although the exact definition of ELLs varies across the United States, these students are typically in the process of learning English and speak a first language other than English at home.

More than half of all ELLs were born in the United States. The National Clearinghouse for English Language Acquisition and Language Instruction Educational Programs (NCELA, 2003) identified the number of English language learners (K–12) in the United States at 4.7 million for 2000–2001. In the 2000 U.S. Census, the question "Do you speak English less than 'very well'?" was answered affirmatively by 8.1 percent of the population. Based on a population of 280 million people, this indicates that almost 23 million people in the United States report that they *do not* speak English well.

Also, according to data from the 2000 U.S. Census, from 1990 to 2000, there was a total population increase of 13.2 percent. Included in that number, 57.9 percent were Hispanic, 48 percent were Asian, and 26 percent were American Indian/Alaskan natives. Similarly, between 1992 and 2002, while the total K–12 enrollment grew 12 percent, English language learners increased by 95 percent (NCELA, 2003).

Changing demographics will continue to have a profound impact on teaching and learning. While some may regard this as a challenge, clearly it can and should be seen as an opportunity. Schools are microcosms of the world. Teachers are working with a more diverse student population perhaps than ever before. We must also face the fact that a paradigm shift has occurred. The notion of one way of teaching to all learners no longer works. One size doesn't fit all! Also of great importance is the fact that teachers are becoming much more introspective, regarding themselves not just as *knowers* but as *facilitators* who can therefore empower students to better understand how they learn best. At the same time, teachers are looking inward to increase self-knowledge as learners. When a teacher acknowledges his or her own learner styles and preferences (and intelligences), there is more likely to be an understanding of strengths and weaknesses in the way one teaches. In other words, do we teach the way *we* learn best?

In *Brain-Compatible Differentiated Instruction for English Language Learners,* you will also find the following:

- National statistics that highlight the faces of diversity in our classrooms
- The impact that No Child Left Behind has on English language learners
- A description of a variety of ESL instructional program models
- An analysis and explanation of brain-compatible theories and the research that underpins this work
- Lesson plan models that demonstrate single-day lesson planning as well as sustained five-day planning
- A discussion of differentiating instruction
- Lesson plan templates and planning grids
- Easy-to-use and adaptable reproducibles
- References to PowerPoint presentations, available on the Pearson website, that accompany major themes and topics covered
- Appendixes with additional resources and materials
- A study guide with questions and activities that can be useful for professional development training (Appendix L)

Brain-Compatible Differentiated Instruction for English Language Learners is divided into three sections. Section One is the theoretical overview, with thirteen topics that contribute to brain-compatible and differentiated teaching and learning and working with English language learners. In Section Two, Planning for Brain-Compatible Differentiated Instruction: One-Day Lessons, you will find five standards-based lessons that accommodate multiple intelligences (MI) and learning styles. Section Three, Planning for Brain-Compatible Differentiated Instruction: Unit Lessons, contains two five-day lessons to give insight into lessons that are to be taught over a period of time—sustained teaching. The thirteen Appendixes contain multiple intelligences activities banks, a lesson plan template, planning grids, a study guide for professional development use, multiple intelligences surveys, and reproducible activities, as well as other resources.

How to Use This Book

How to Read the Lesson Plans

The introduction to each unit or single-day plan highlights research that underpins the topic and should be read first because it is vital to understand how and why something works in the classroom. The Before You Begin section gives cues as to what materials are needed and any prior preparations that should be made.

Next is the following information:

1. A real-life classroom scenario and program model. Program models (described in more detail later) in which these lessons might work best are identified, although this should not be limiting. Clearly these lessons and units may work equally as well for mainstream educators with ELLs in their classrooms.
2. The appropriate TESOL standards and the Virginia *Standards of Learning* (SOLs) found at www.doe.Virginia.gov/VDOE/Instruction/sol.html. The Virginia *Standards of Learning* are referred to in this book because I teach in Virginia. Visit your state's department of education website to find similar standards that apply to your state.
3. Alignment with the No Child Left Behind legislation.
4. A list of the intelligences and learning styles accommodated in the lesson.

The first section of the lesson plan is the *planning phase,* which contains *content* and *language objectives.* This is followed by space to identify *materials* needed. The lessons provided in this book require various resources, such as paper, markers, posters, and charts. Most are readily available to you and do not require any additional expense. Some lessons require the use of educational videos. Check to see if your school subscribes to United Streaming Video (http://unitedstreaming.com). This is an excellent resource! If your school does not subscribe, do not hesitate to look online for other free videos.

Next is the topic or content vocabulary. An expanded vocabulary list will come later in the plan. The *teaching phase* includes the warm-up activity, transition, and a description of the activities. The five English language proficiency levels are delineated to show how to differentiate for each student who matches a particular profile. The types of assessment highlight either formal or informal, formative or summative. The plan concludes with a closure activity that suggests how to end the lesson. The *conclusion* describes why and how this lesson can be effectively and successfully executed. The homework further extends the lesson by asking students to engage in additional tasks that directly relate to the material being covered.

Additionally, each plan is accompanied by a vocabulary list and a sample performance indicator. Sample performance indicators include the following:

- Examples of how to operationalize the English language proficiency standards
- Expected performance at the end of a given level of language proficiency
- Ideas for scaffolding or differentiating language instruction
- Flexible and dynamic elements, intended to be combined across standards or language domains or interchanged or substituted according to contexts of instruction

What If Factors

These are included to help demonstrate that teaching requires a great deal of flexibility and to remind us that we must plan for the expected and unexpected.

Teacher's Reflection

At the end of each lesson is a place to highlight the impact of the lesson and the teacher's reflective comments about what worked well in addition to the challenges presented.

Theory to Practice

These are citations that further illustrate the theoretical underpinnings of each lesson.

Glossary of Terms

This is provided for the reader to help define any new terminology used in this lesson.

Reproducible Activities

Appendix M contains reproducible activities and a vocabulary list for each lesson that can easily be copied and used.

Now It's Your Turn!

These questions provide opportunities for self-reflection and interaction with the topics being covered.

Questions for Discussion

These further elucidate ideas or suggestions about this lesson that might be considered.

If you are a beginning teacher, you may find it very helpful to have planning units already done for you. However, as you will quickly discover, you should feel free to explore what works best for you and your students. These units can be modified accordingly.

In Appendixes B and C there are brain-compatible differentiated instruction for English language learners planning grids for you to practice creating a lesson. There is also a lesson plan template in Appendix A to practice creating your own lesson based on the sample lessons provided. Other appendixes include a tool kit of multiple intelligences and standards-based instruction for English language learners. These reproducibles, also referred to as *blackline masters,* will provide extra information and activities as you continue to build a teaching repertoire. You will also find a sampling of multiple intelligences surveys (Appendixes J and K) that you may wish to use with your students. These are *not* diagnostic or prescriptive. They should be administered with your students as a fun way to help them begin to recognize the many ways in which they are smart! Try them at multiple points throughout your school year. Remember, it is important that students realize that they have *multiple* intelligences and they should not focus just on their strengths. Also included are MI activities banks (Appendixes E and F).

Of particular interest are the study guide questions in Appendix L. Across the United States school districts are adopting books such as this one and using them for professional development activities. The guide provides you with ideas and options for utilizing these questions as a beneficial resource.

There are thirteen PowerPoint presentations on various topics covered in the lessons that further illustrate additional information on highly successful ways to work with ELLs. Throughout the book you will see an icon in the margin, indicating that this PowerPoint provides more background on a certain topic. I encourage you to start with the PowerPoint titled "Brain-Compatible Differentiated Instruction," because it sets the stage for the book and helps facilitate your interactive work with peers or colleagues. The following lists the PowerPoints and their contents:

- *Brain-Compatible Differentiated Instruction.* Offers a broad introductory perspective of the book. Included are five activities that allow you to engage with topics that include descriptions of differentiated instruction, an outline of Howard Gardner's theory of multiple intelligences, definitions of learning styles, tools for the differentiated classroom, lesson planning and assessment, and samples of instructional practices.

- *Standards-Based Planning.* Provides basic questions that should be posed in order to determine how to proceed with the planning process. These are followed by a series of questions that address creating instructional activities. Answering these questions enables the classroom teacher to create a road map for long- and short-term planning.

- *Assessment for ELLs.* Demonstrates easy-to-follow directions for assessing students while conducting classroom observations.

- *Solid Teaching Strategies.* Highlights a listing of teaching strategies that are highly successful with ELLs. These include both verbal and nonverbal cueing and gesturing. Special attention is paid to giving directions and rate of speech.

- *Differentiating Instruction.* Explains differentiating instruction in an interactive format. Clarifies in pertinent details what it is and isn't; why, when, and how to differentiate; and gives specific examples of what a differentiated classroom looks like. Additional online resources are provided.

- *Second Language Acquisition.* Illustrates second language acquisition as a process usually involving five stages. Each stage is clearly defined and factors that determine progression are delineated.

- *Valuing Diverse Students.* Introduces the WGBH video library, *Teaching Foreign Languages.* While this resource is intended for foreign/world language teachers, it is useful for all teachers to view and understand the pedagogical implications of working with culturally, linguistically, and cognitively diverse learners.

- *Scaffolding.* Provides a simplistic explanation of what and how to scaffold instruction and assessment. Specific examples are given to suggest ways this is evidenced in the classroom. Attention is given to helping beginning ELLs.

- *Creating Transitions in the Classroom.* Demonstrates easy-to-follow steps for creating transitions in a daily lesson plan. Explanations are given on how to connect several activities, beginning with the warm-up, thus providing a "seamless" teaching and learning experience.

- *How Languages Are Learned and Acquired.* Features an in-depth overview of language learning and language acquisition as an interactive approach to teaching and learning. Explores the interactive roles of first (L1) and second (L2) language as seen through the lenses of sociocultural and psycholinguistic theories.

- *Demographic Changes—New Challenges and Opportunities!* Highlights data that indicate the impact on U.S. schools of changing demographics and the challenges and opportunities that result. Suggestions are made for bridging schools and communities through various kinds of partnerships as well as ways to enhance parental involvement.

- *Story-Based Approach to Teaching Grammar.* Focuses on teaching grammar through the use of storytelling. The PACE model is outlined and explained as an effective tool for teaching grammar. Included are steps for designing a contextualized story-based lesson.

- *No Child Left Behind.*   Explains the federal law affecting education from kindergarten through high school. Key elements of NCLB as well as objectives for professional development, expectations for schools, and clarification of Title I and Title II are included.

The PowerPoints are available on the accompanying website, www.pearsonhighered.com/educator.

Acknowledgments

I would like to offer my heartfelt thanks to all the ESL pre- and in-service teachers who were so enthusiastic in contributing their ideas and suggestions: Amanda Seewald, Maracas Program (NJ); Sandra J. Fraser, Fairfax County Public Schools (VA); Tracey E. Brooks, George Mason University (VA); MiMi Granados, Fairfax County Public Schools (VA); Delia Racines, Fairfax County Public Schools (VA); Kim Inge, International Schools (People's Republic of China); Lori S. Freidman, George Mason University (VA); Melissa Ferro, George Mason University (VA); Fu Li, George Mason University (VA); and Rebecca Upchurch, Fairfax County Public Schools (VA).

Melissa Ferro and Fu Li worked tirelessly as graduate assistants to ensure that the manuscript met the standard we set. I greatly appreciate your commitment. I am particularly grateful to Amanda Seewald for all her efforts but most importantly, for sharing my passion and vision for this work.

I also thank the following reviewers: Deborah A. Carr, Hazleton Area School District; Lisa J. DeMaagd, Taft Elementary; Linda Lippitt, New Mexico Highlands University; Gerald McCain, Southern Oregon University; Paul H. Matthews, University of Georgia; Judith B. O'Loughlin, New Jersey City University; Patti D. Pettigrew, California State University San Marcos; Adrean Rivers-Horan, Remington Elementary School; Kathy Schmitz, St. Petersburg College; and Yvonne D. Taylor, Shippensburg University.

A special thanks to my big sis, Millie, who nursed me through my recovery after my riding accident! Without a doubt I must thank my daughter, Esther, and best friends Janice (whose tireless efforts with editing were so appreciated) and Robin, who were always there with words of encouragement. Finally, thanks to my horses, Floyd and Freestate—just being around you and going for rides keeps me balanced!

Brain-Compatible Differentiated Instruction for English Language Learners

INTRODUCTION

How to Plan for Brain-Compatible Differentiated Instruction

Using the Lesson Plan Template

The lesson plan template provided in Appendix A and used in the lessons in Sections Two and Three is presented section by section in this Introduction. It is designed to be comprehensive and should be very useful, especially for a beginning teacher. Note that I do not necessarily define a lesson as one class period. Rather, I define it based on the objectives that have been determined for that particular lesson, and it may extend over several class periods.

Sample Lesson Plan Template
(English as a Second Language)

Teacher _____ School _____

Grade(s) _____ Proficiency Level(s) _____ Program Model _____

Content _____

PLANNING PHASE

Content and/or Language Objectives
As a result of this lesson, students will be able to:

1. _____
2. _____
3. _____

Vocabulary

Materials

Lesson Outline

Content _____

National/State/Local Standards _____

TEACHING PHASE SEQUENCE

Warm-Up Activity

Transition

Activities

Grouping	Scaffolding	Processes
Entire class	Modeling	Reading
Small group	Individual	Listening
Partners	Guided	Writing
Individual		Individual

Activity 1

Activity 2

Activity 3

Differentiated Instruction
Starting Up
Beginning
Developing
Expanding
Bridging

Assessment

Closure
Review of this lesson
Preview for next lesson

Homework

REFLECTION PHASE

Learning Objectives
Were the content and/or language objectives met? How or why not?

Efforts to Accommodate:
Visual learners _____
Auditory learners _____
Tactile learners _____
Specials needs learners _____

What worked well?
What didn't work well?
What will you do differently as a result of this plan?
How might this lesson be improved?
The important thing I learned was _____

First, the teacher is identified, as are grade(s) of students, proficiency levels, content, and program model. These factors are typically referred to as *demographic information.*

Sample Lesson Plan Template
(English as a Second Language)

Teacher _____ School _____

Grade(s) _____ Proficiency Level(s) _____ Program Model _____

Content _____

Standards-Based
Planning

Next, the *planning phase* is outlined. Here the teacher clearly and succinctly lists the lesson's content and language objectives, vocabulary, and materials. This is also where the teacher describes the subject-area content and identifies the lesson's alignment with national, state, and/or local standards.

Lesson objectives play a vital role in the overall instructional plan. Writing the lesson's objectives requires you to understand what is to be taught, to whom, and under what circumstances. Once you are familiar with national, state, and local standards and understand the curriculum, sometimes referred to as the program of study (POS) to be taught, planning brain-compatible differentiated instruction is a straightforward task. When planning instruction for English language learners (ELLs), the most beneficial approach to writing objectives encompasses both content and language. Also, keeping in mind that most states now require proficiency exams for ELLs, lessons must be planned around emphasizing the four skills of listening, speaking, reading, and writing.

Content objectives, which identify what students should know and be able to do, guide teaching and learning. The bottom line for English learners is that content objectives need to be written in terms of what students will learn or do, stated simply, orally and in writing, and tied to specific grade-level content standards (Echevarria & Graves, 2007). Content objectives are usually taken from the state core subject-area standards. Some verbs that typically describe content objectives include *create, distinguish, select, identify,* and *solve.* For example, *Students will be able to name, describe, and order the planets* (see Lesson 1).

While carefully planning to accomplish content objectives, teachers must also incorporate in their lesson plans activities that support students' language development (Short, 1999). As with content objectives, *language objectives* should be stated clearly and simply, and students should be informed of them, both orally and in writing (Echevarria, Vogt, & Short, 2008). Verbs used for language objectives include *write, compare, define, retell,* and *summarize.* For example, *Students will be able to compare and contrast what an animal cell and a plant cell look like, their functions, and their main differences in structure using a Venn diagram graphic organizer* (see Lesson 3).

PLANNING PHASE

Content and/or Language Objectives
As a result of this lesson, students will be able to:

1. _____

2. _____

3. _____

Vocabulary

Materials

Lesson Outline

Content _____

National/State/Local Standards _____

The next section is called the *teaching phase sequence.* The opening activity, the *warm-up,* is a vital start to the beginning of every class, focusing learners on moving from the external variables of school life to concentrate on the start of a new learning experience for that day.

Creating Transitions in the Classroom

Next comes a *transition* to the main parts of the lesson. See any of the lessons in Section Two for examples. Although specified here, transitions are used throughout the lesson to provide seamless connections between each activity. Next, to help you decide how to balance your teaching, the *activities* grid enables you to utilize *grouping, scaffolding,* and multiple *processes,* as noted. Simply placing a check mark allows you to see at a glance how varied your teaching strategies are. Following this is the *activities* section, in which you describe the activities that comprise the lesson. The number of activities can be increased or reduced as needed. In the next section you will describe *differentiated instruction* for the TESOL (Teachers of English to Speakers of Other Languages) five levels of proficiency. Finally, this part of the template includes spaces for *assessment, closure,* and a description of *homework.*

Homework should be an extension of the day's activities. However, keep in mind that some students will not have someone at home to give assistance. We should also not take for granted that students will have access to a variety of resources (i.e., Internet, newspapers, or even books). Homework must be given with clear directions and purpose. It is always a good idea to check that students understand the assignment before they leave the classroom.

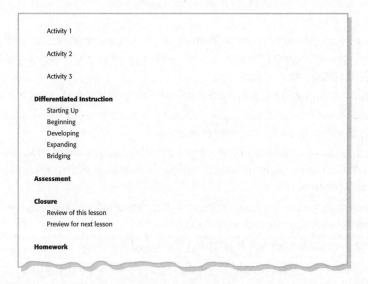

TEACHING PHASE SEQUENCE

Warm-up Activity

Transition

Activities

Grouping	Scaffolding	Processes
Entire class	Modeling	Reading
Small group	Individual	Listening
Partners	Guided	Writing
Individual		Individual

Activity 1

Activity 2

Activity 3

Differentiated Instruction
Starting Up
Beginning
Developing
Expanding
Bridging

Assessment

Closure
Review of this lesson
Preview for next lesson

Homework

The last section of the lesson plan template is just as important as the planning and teaching phases. The *reflection phase* gives you an opportunity to examine your practice introspectively, allowing multiple opportunities for reflective practice. Reflective practice is a conscious, systematic, deliberate process of framing and reframing classroom practice, in light of the consequential actions, democratic principles, educational beliefs, values, and preferred visions teachers bring to the teaching–learning event (Serrafini, 2002). You are strongly encouraged to use this section to reflect on what is working well and what is not. Doing so allows you to decide what adjustments you may wish to make. This also gives you the opportunity to look at your teaching through multiple lenses and make informed decisions about your practice.

REFLECTION PHASE

Learning Objectives
Were the content and/or language objectives met? How or why not?

Efforts to Accommodate:
Visual learners _____
Auditory learners _____
Tactile learners _____
Specials needs learners _____

What worked well? _____
What didn't work well? _____
What will you do differently as a result of this plan? _____
How might this lesson be improved? _____
One important thing I learned was _____

Guidelines for Creating Lesson Plans

1. Determine what your local and state curricula require you to teach. Identify the content and/or language objectives.
2. Decide what vocabulary is to be taught along with a strategy for preteaching new words.
3. Have materials, resources, and supplies readily available and well organized for easy access.
4. Determine what students need to know (facts and information), to understand (principles and concepts), and to do (summarize or retell) as a result of the learning experience.
5. Identify national, state, and local standards with which to align your lessons.
6. Decide what differentiated needs the students have based on pre- or posttests and other formal or informal assessments.
7. Determine which strategy or strategies of differentiated instruction you want to use. Examples might include grouping, scaffolding, tiered assignments, or learning centers.
8. Decide how you will use assessments (formal and informal) to engage all learners' intelligences and learning styles.
9. Make sure the homework is purposeful and has meaning.

References

Echevarria, J., & Graves, A. (2007). *Sheltered content instruction: Teaching English language learners with diverse abilities* (3rd ed.). Boston: Allyn & Bacon.

Echevarria, J., Vogt, M., & Short, D. (2008). *Making content comprehensible for English learners* (3rd ed.). Boston: Allyn & Bacon.

National Clearinghouse for English Language Acquisition and Language Instruction Educational Programs. (2003). *The growing numbers of limited English proficient students 1991/1992–2001/02.* Washington, DC: NCELA.

Serrafini, F. (2002). Three paradigms of assessment: Measurement, procedure, and inquiry. *The Reading Teacher, 54*(4), 384–393.

Short, D. (1999). Integrating language and content for effective sheltered instruction programs. In C. Faltis & P. Wolfe (Eds.), *So much to say: Adolescents, bilingualism, and ESL in the secondary school* (pp. 105–137). New York: Teachers College Press.

Standard & Poor's. SchoolDataDirect. (n.d.) School demographics: How many English language learners are in our schools? Retrieved July 16, 2008, from www.centerforpubliceducation.org/site

Teachers of English to Speakers of Other Languages. (2006). *PreK–12 English language proficiency standards.* Alexandria, VA: TESOL.

SECTION ONE

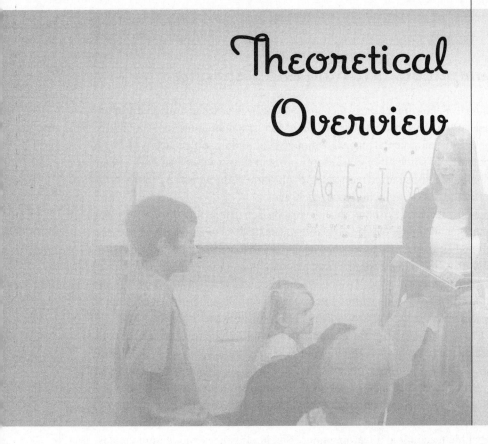

Theoretical Overview

In order to better understand important concepts about brain-compatible teaching and learning and differentiating instruction for ELLs, this section provides thirteen topics that all contribute to successful instructional practices. Starting with a definition of *brain-compatible teaching and learning,* you will be introduced to *brain-compatible theories of teaching and learning* that substantiate the validity of this work as they relate to multiple intelligences and learning styles. Once you have examined *differentiating instruction* and how to use such strategies as anchor activities and structures, you will see how these are portrayed in the lessons provided.

Meeting the needs of English language learners covers methods to ensure the success of culturally and linguistically diverse learners. The effects of *No Child Left Behind* are discussed. Next, TESOL's *ESL Standards for Pre-K–12 Students and English Language Proficiency Standards* are detailed as well as the *TESOL performance indicators and how to read them.* Also discussed are the *World-Class Instructional Design and Assessment (WIDA)* CAN DO Descriptors, followed by an overview of *second language acquisition theory* that details two of James Cummins's theoretical models.

You will also find definitions of various *program models of instruction* used in the United States, many of which are highlighted in the sample lessons. Among the numerous methods that are highly effective, two popular *methods of instruction* used with ELLs are covered: Cognitive Academic Language Learning Approach (CALLA) and Total Physical Response (TPR). These were selected because they are brain friendly and widely used in teaching English language learners.

Classroom management stresses the distinction between classroom management and discipline. Topics covered include forming groups, centers, seating arrangements, managing large classes, and establishing rules and nonverbal cues. A discussion of *classroom discipline* ends this section.

Brain-Compatible Teaching and Learning

What is brain-compatible teaching? Brain teaching emphasizes how the brain learns naturally and is based on what we currently know about the actual structures and functions of the brain at several developmental stages. Although brain-compatible teaching is not a panacea or magic bullet to solve all of education's problems, as teachers we must understand certain principles and use effective strategies in purposeful ways. In other words, we must understand the reasoning behind our teaching.

Brain-compatible learning is a comprehensive approach to teaching that uses current research from neuroscience fields. We are now able to use the latest neuroscience research to create instructional strategies and assessment practices that are brain friendly and provide a biologically driven paradigm for effective teaching and learning.

During the past twenty years neuroscientists have conducted research that has important implications for improved teaching, due in large part to a better understanding of how the brain works. With just a cursory understanding of how the brain functions, we can better assist ELLs. Brain-compatible teaching offers multimodal and sensory ways to approach all learners. Given what we know about learner differences, brain-compatible teaching provides tools for learning, problem solving, and creating. In this book you will find ways to empower students to understand how they learn. When individuals have opportunities to learn through their strengths, unexpected and positive cognitive, emotional, and social changes will appear.

Brain-compatible teaching and learning addresses intelligences and learning styles, with the focus placed on the student as an individual. As educators we must plan lessons and assessments that enable and empower students, structured in ways that allow all students to reach their full potential. When students enter our classrooms, they should feel that every opportunity will be afforded them to succeed. Students are recognized as lifelong learners and encouraged to draw on their background knowledge and linguistic and cultural experiences to use as tools in their continued development. When teaching and assessment practices reflect the diverse students in our classrooms today, success is inevitable.

Brain-Compatible Theories of Teaching and Learning

Gardner's Theory of Multiple Intelligences

According to Howard Gardner's theory of multiple intelligences (MI), there are eight intelligences: bodily/kinesthetic, interpersonal/social, intrapersonal/introspective, logical/mathematical, musical/rhythmic, naturalist, verbal/linguistic, and visual/spatial. Every learner has the capacity to exhibit all of these intelligences, but some are more highly developed than others in most individuals. Based on MI theory, the challenge in education is for teachers to create learning environments that foster the development of *all* eight intelligences. Balanced instructional presentations that encourage addressing the multiple intelligences benefit all learners and expose students to the appropriate means through which they can strengthen their underutilized intelligences. However, Gardner did not offer very much practical advice on classroom applications of his theory. His seminal work on this subject, *Frames of Mind* (1983), devotes over 300 pages to explaining and differentiating what were then conceived as six intelligences, but only two chapters, or 60 pages, are concerned with the implications and applications of MI theory in education.

One defense of Gardner's theory is presented in the article "Where Do the Learning Theories Overlap?" (Guild, 1997). The author compares the key features and principles of three learning theories: multiple intelligences, learning styles, and brain-based education. He concludes that these theories intersect significantly, particularly in terms of their intended results. One point in common is that these theories are learner centered. Another similarity is the teacher's role as reflective practitioner and facilitator, with the student acting as a reflective partner. An additional mutual theme is the concern for the education of the whole person. All three theories emphasize curricula with depth and breadth. Additionally, MI theory, learning styles, and brain-based education promote diversity and inclusiveness rather than the "lowest common denominator" approach to teaching. These three approaches focus on how students learn differently, acknowledging that the "more diverse learning experiences we provide our students, the more robust their education will be, the more ways they will learn each topic, hence the more they are prepared to succeed in a world marked by increasing diversity and an accelerating change rate" (Haley, 2001).

The literature on multiple intelligences provides a sound theoretical foundation for an integrated, multidimensional style of education across learning styles and cultures. Moreover, since Gardner first announced his theory of multiple intelligences, many books, professional papers, and journal articles have been published to fill the perceived gap in field research related to classroom lesson planning based on the theory. One example, *Multiple Intelligences: Multiple Ways to Help Students Learn Foreign Languages* (Gahala & Lange, 1997) notes, "Teaching with multiple intelligences is a way of taking differences among students seriously, sharing that knowledge with students and parents, guiding students in taking responsibility for their own learning, and presenting worthwhile materials that maximize learning and understanding" (p. 91).

A second example is *Teaching and Learning Languages through Multiple Intelligences* (Christison, 1996). MI theory offers ESL/English as a Foreign Language (EFL) teachers a way to examine their best teaching techniques and strategies in light of human differences. There are two important steps to follow in understanding how MI theory applies to teaching English as a second language. The first step is to identify activities that we frequently use in our classes and categorize them. The second step is to track what we are doing with multiple intelligences. The following list applies to verbal/linguistic intelligence, but the same procedure with different specifics could apply to any of them.

1. *Awaken the intelligence.* Lesson begins with a riddle or brain teaser. The teacher divides students into groups and gives each one a series of riddles. The students then work collaboratively to solve the riddles.
2. *Amplify the intelligence.* Practice with the awakened intelligence and it will improve. Students practice describing commonly known objects.
3. *Teach for/with the intelligence.* Students describe objects in a large-group discussion.
4. *Transfer the intelligence.* Help students reflect on their learning in the previous stages and help them make the lesson content relevant to their lives outside the classroom.

A third example is a pilot study I conducted (Haley, 2001). The purpose of the study was to identify, document, and promote effective real-world applications of MI theory in foreign and second-language classrooms. Results indicated that teachers were profoundly affected by these approaches. They felt that their teaching experienced a shift in paradigm to a more learner-centered classroom; they were once again energized and enthusiastic about their pedagogy, and they felt they were able to reach more students. Students demonstrated keen interest in MI concepts and showed positive responses to the increased variety of instructional strategies used in their foreign language/ESL classrooms.

Providing opportunities for students to learn in ways to which they are most receptive maximizes their potential for success in the academic setting and in real life. Integrating multiple intelligences into the classroom setting does not require a major overhaul of teaching methodology or a total revamping of adopted curricula. In general, supplementing and revising existing lesson plans with creative and innovative ideas will suffice. Thematic and interdisciplinary units that provide cooperative learning and that include a variety of tasks accomplished through a choice of activities allow for multiple intelligences to be well represented within the context of instruction. Both Glasgow (1996) and Glasgow and Bush (1996) emphasize classroom use and real-world applications of such lessons. Relating the eight intelligences to future career choices is especially valuable.

How to Identify the Intelligences of Students with Language and Cultural Differences

Identifying students' intelligences is an ongoing process. While everyone has all eight intelligences, we should recognize that we have them to varying degrees and that these change over time. Therefore, when working with ELLs, you are responsible for knowing about your students' backgrounds to help you understand behaviors demonstrated in the classroom. However, be careful not to stereotype students. This is a dangerous pitfall and should be avoided at all cost. It is important to be an astute observer so that when you have taken the time to learn about your students' backgrounds (language, culture, literacy, etc.), you can determine the strengths and weaknesses of their various intelligences. For beginning students with little to no spoken or written language, you must rely on visual support, acting out, mime, nonverbal cues, or when available, the use of a translator. As students progress and gain higher levels of proficiency, interviews and surveys can be used. (See the surveys in Appendixes J and K).

Building on the Strengths of Multiple Intelligences While Working with English Language Learners

Integrating the theory of multiple intelligences into daily planning affords learners multi-modal (paired, groups, individual, teacher centered, student centered) and multisensory (visual, auditory, kinesthetic) approaches to language development and content comprehension. In other words, planning activities that incorporate abilities accommodating the various intelligences provides students multiple opportunities for success. *Finding Out/ Descubrimiento* (De Avila & Duncan, 1980) is an example of an elementary math and science curriculum that incorporates multiple intelligences.

In 1997, I began reading and investigating research on Howard Gardner's theory of multiple intelligences. As I worked with teachers and my own graduate students while exploring the feasibility of implementing MI theory in foreign and second language classes, I became more and more convinced that this truly is a way to empower *all* learners. Each time I visit a school where teachers are including aspects of MI theory in their instructional strategies and assessment programs, I continue to be amazed at how powerful and successful this can be for both novice and veteran teachers.

The chart on page 12 includes MI characteristics and activities that you can easily adapt in your classroom teaching. When planning, first determine how many of the intelligences will be utilized in completing an activity. The answer provides an accounting of how many opportunities are given for students to succeed. If you are only using two or three intelligences, many learners will be denied access to demonstrating what they know and understand. On page 13 is a sample MI survey for teachers. Before you continue reading, take the survey and calculate your score. This may help enhance your skills as a reflective practitioner and provide some insight on how your own intelligences impact your teaching.

It is important to distinguish between multiple intelligences and learning styles. While they each share some characteristics, it is helpful to think of them in terms of how learners demonstrate proclivity and preference. In other words, intelligences are believed to be determined at birth, while learning styles can usually be taught, depending on the learner's attitude and motivation toward the subject matter.

The next section further explains learning styles and how they are recognized and accommodated in classrooms with English language learners.

Learning Styles

Have you ever wondered why some people learn best by seeing, or by hearing, or by performing a physical activity? These different approaches to learning are personal preferences and they help define who we are as individuals. Learning styles are simply different approaches or ways of learning. The more we understand "how" students learn best, the better equipped we are to provide instruction and assessment practices that maximize learning outcomes. There are basically three types of learning styles: visual, auditory, and kinesthetic. It is especially important for you to understand your own learning styles and tailor teaching in ways that incorporate a variety of learning styles demonstrated by your students. It is also important for you as a teacher to be aware of your own preferred learning styles as these can and do influence the way we teach. Understanding our own strengths and weaknesses prevents us from teaching just to our strengths, therefore running the risk of precluding success for the diversity of students in our classes.

Some English language learners use learning styles that are a result of previous schooling. Some students have been taught to learn by means of rote memory; others have been taught to observe closely until it is their turn to do something by themselves (Balderrama & Díaz-Rico, 2006). In many Western cultures, learning by doing is emphasized, and trial and error is preferred over a more passive approach (Helmer & Eddy, 2003). Teachers may observe that some students feel more confident with direct instruction accompanied by rote memorization. Others blurt out answers or compete for a chance to answer, whereas still others speak only in small-group settings (Balderrama & Díaz-Rico, 2006).

Learning styles are the general approaches—for example, global or analytic, auditory or visual—that students use in acquiring a new language or in learning any other subject (Oxford, 2003, p. 2). These styles are the "overall patterns that give general direction to learning behavior" (Cornett, 1983, p. 9).

Ehrman and Oxford (1989) cited five major style dimensions relevant to English language learning: sensory preferences, personality types, extroverted versus introverted, intuitive–random versus sensing–sequential, and thinking versus feeling. The activities included in this book focus on one dimension of learning styles that are likely to work well with English language learners—sensory preferences. Sensory preferences refer to the physical, perceptual learning channels with which the student is the most comfortable (Oxford, 2003, p. 3).

As a classroom teacher, it is critically important to provide instruction that encompasses different learning styles. There are several potentially highly effective teaching strategies that you may wish to consider. To begin this process, it is often a good idea to start with an assessment tool for making such determinations. You may choose to use a

Solid Teaching
Strategies

Multiple Intelligences—Activities and Characteristics

INTELLIGENCE	ACTIVITIES	CHARACTERISTICS
Verbal/Linguistic	Creative writing/journal writing. Storytelling. Oral debate/presentations. Reading.	Understands order and meanings of words. Explains and teaches well. Demonstrates memory and recall.
Musical/Rhythmic	Jazz chants. Music composition. Rhythm and percussion activities. Singing/humming. Musical performance.	Does well in drama, aerobic alphabet/exercise, mime, and sports. Can discern tones and pitch.
Logical/Mathematical	Using graphic organizers. Formulas/number sequences. Pattern games. Problem solving. Deciphering codes.	Enjoys abstract pattern recognition or inductive/deductive reasoning. Discerns relationships. Does complex calculations.
Visual/Spatial	Painting/drawing. Patterns and designs. Using various forms of multimedia. Sculpture/pictures. Mind mapping.	Creates graphic representations, image manipulation, mental pictures, and images. Displays active imagination.
Bodily/Kinesthetic	Dancing, acting, running. Playing sports. Processing knowledge with body motion.	Enjoys dancing. Role plays. Likes drama. Does well in sports. Prefers to use manipulatives.
Naturalist	Drawing or photographing a natural setting. Describing changes in the local environment. Planning a campaign which focuses on endangered animals.	Enjoys flora, fauna, and other natural phenomena. Appreciates impact of nature on self and self on nature.
Intrapersonal/Introspective	Silent reflection. Thinking strategies. Complex guided imagery. Self-paced independent work.	Relates to inner states of being. Self-reflective. Is aware and can express feelings. Displays higher-order thinking/reasoning.
Interpersonal/Social	Giving/receiving feedback. Cooperative learning. One-to-one communication. Group projects.	Discerns underlying intentions, behavior, and perspectives of another. Works cooperatively in groups. Is sensitive to others' feelings, moods, and motives. Excels in verbal/nonverbal communication skills.

Teachers' Intelligences Survey

Write the number that comes closest to reflecting your intelligences:
1 = Almost never   2 = Sometimes   3 = Nearly always

1. _____ I hear words in my head before I read, speak, or write them.

2. _____ Learning languages other than my mother tongue comes easily to me.

3. _____ When giving directions to students I tend to model with a graphic representation.

4. _____ My classroom is purposely decorated and arranged so that it is visually stimulating.

5. _____ I prefer to move around during class rather than sit or stand in one place.

6. _____ I participate in at least one sport or physical activity on a regular basis.

7. _____ I frequently use teacher-centered methods to teach.

8. _____ My mind searches for patterns and regularities in things when I am explaining new concepts to my students.

9. _____ Music is a very important part of my teaching repertoire.

10. _____ Particular musical passages bring memories and mental images to me.

11. _____ My students often come to me for advice.

12. _____ I am regarded as a leader in my school.

13. _____ I am happy with the way I have taken advantage of life's opportunities.

14. _____ I keep a personal diary or journal to write down my thoughts and feelings about teaching and life in general.

15. _____ I have a garden and/or like to work outdoors.

16. _____ It's easy for me to tell the difference between various kinds of plants and animals.

Add the total scores for your responses in each of the intelligences.

	TOTAL
Verbal/Linguistic: 1, 2	_____
Visual/Spatial: 3, 4	_____
Bodily/Kinesthetic: 5, 6	_____
Logical/Mathematical: 7, 8	_____
Musical/Rhythmic: 9, 10	_____
Interpersonal/Social: 11, 12	_____
Intrapersonal/Introspective: 13, 14	_____
Naturalist: 15, 16	_____

Analysis of Scores
1–2 = Not a strong area   3–4 = Area of comfort   5–6 = Area of strength

written survey on which students answer questions about their preferred way(s) of learning. The following recommended websites may be helpful:

www.ldpride.net/learningstyles.MI.htm

www.berghuis.com.nz/abiator/lsi/lisframe.html

www.learning-styles-online.com/inventory

www.vark-learn.com/english/index.asp

www.everythingesl.net/inservices/learningstyle.php

The following chart represents the learning styles highlighted in this book.

LEARNING STYLE	ACTIVITIES	CHARACTERISTICS
Visual	Using assistive technologies. Painting/drawing. Mind mapping and graphic organizers.	Learns through seeing.
Auditory	Storytelling. Oral debate or presentations. Morning Message. Read-aloud activities. Audio books.	Learns through listening.
Kinesthetic	Role playing. Simulations. Total Physical Response or Total Physical Response Storytelling.	Learns through doing, moving, touching.

Working with Nonspeakers of English and Beginners

It is very important that as the teacher you model how to complete tasks. Providing graphic organizers (see Lesson 3) and meaningful visuals to support lessons will greatly assist *all* students and especially nonspeakers of English and beginners. Until you have determined students' learning styles it is also useful to appropriately modulate language delivery—speed and enunciation—when modeling language forms or presenting content. Repetition helps. Sample activities might include vocabulary journals, A-B-C books, word webs, and word walls.

Learning about Your Students through Observation

As mentioned earlier, it is important to be an astute observer. This enables the teacher to discover *how* students learn. For instance if there are students who seem to grasp concepts more easily if allowed to feel, touch, and manipulate items, that indicates that these students may be kinesthetic learners (see Lessons 1 and 4). Often these students may not perform well on traditional paper-and-pencil tests. However, they know and understand the material being taught. Through careful observations, you can therefore provide multimodal and multisensory approaches to instruction and assessment. In other words, allow students to show what they know.

This is also good to remember when giving directions. Many ELLs will need to "see" directions printed as well as hear them given orally. Students are still making connections between sounds, intonation, timbre, and pitch. Even if they are not literate in either the home language (L1) or second language (L2), they begin to develop preliteracy skills for word and sound recognition.

Pay careful attention to how students follow directions. Notice the sequence of their work habits. Are some students more inclined to ask for help before attempting a task independently? You can easily keep notes (both written and mental) and guide instruction and assessment accordingly. What is most important is the awareness that all students will demonstrate preferred learning styles and these may vary from day to day.

Differentiating Instruction

In addition to acknowledging that planning must include recognition of diverse students, as teachers we must also be aware that students learn at different speeds and that they differ widely in their abilities to think abstractly or understand complex ideas. How do you divide your time, resources, and efforts to effectively instruct all students with diverse backgrounds, readiness levels, skill levels, interests, and ways of learning? This is even more challenging when we consider the range of proficiency levels that you will encounter when teaching ELLs. How can you be expected to plan for reaching *all* learners? According to Tomlinson (2000):

Differentiating
Instruction

> There is no contradiction between effective standards-based instruction and differentiation. Curriculum tells us *what* to teach: Differentiation tells us *how.* Thus, if we elect to teach a standards-based curriculum, differentiation simply suggests ways in which we can make that curriculum work best for varied learners. In other words, differentiation can show us how to teach the same standard to a range of learners by employing a variety of teaching and learning modes. (p. 7)

In Tomlinson's (1999) book, *The Differentiated Classroom: Responding to the Needs of ALL Learners,* she provides multiple descriptions and examples of teachers at work creating differentiated classrooms. She stresses the importance of the teacher being a guide and facilitator who accommodates student differences.

According to Tomlinson, there are three aspects of differentiating:

1. *Content.* Concepts, principles, and skills that teachers want students to learn
2. *Process.* Activities that help students make sense of, and come to own, the ideas and skills being taught
3. *Products.* Culminating projects that allow students to demonstrate and extend what they have learned

Planning differed instruction while meeting national, state, and local standards *is* possible. It takes careful thought and deliberation. If you are a beginning teacher you may want to seek advice from a mentor or senior teacher if things seem to be a bit overwhelming at first. Remember, what is most important is that you approach every class and every individual student as separate and unique. Get to know your students—their backgrounds, interests, and experiences. Value the diversity of learners you teach and take your students where they are and work with them to reach their full potential.

Valuing Diverse
Students

How do you ensure that all learners are accommodated? Ideas in the accompanying guidelines box can help you strategize for differentiated instruction.

Guidelines for Differentiating Instruction

1. Start to differentiate at a pace that works best for you.
2. Determine your rationale for differentiating instruction.
3. Select assessment tools to decide what and who needs differentiated instruction.
4. Place emphasis on students taking responsibility for their own learning where possible.
5. Create opportunities to plan with other teachers for optimal success.
6. Plan lessons that balance student- and teacher-centered instruction based on readiness levels, interest, intelligences, and learning styles. Allow choices for some activities.
7. Communicate with parents to explain differentiated instruction and assessment and their benefits.

As you continue to develop instructional strategies that accommodate diverse students, the following two activity structures provide additional ways to differentiate instruction and assessment.

Differentiating Instruction and Anchor Activities

We know that not all students learn at the same pace. When some students are ready to move on, a differentiated instruction strategy called Anchors can offer enrichment and deeper meaning to their learning. Anchors are specifically designed activities that aid in deepening student understanding of content while enhancing language skills. These should not be regarded as busy work. They offer meaningful work for students when they finish an assignment or project. Providing students with options in learning activities can increase student achievement and engagement. Anchor activities help meet varying student intelligences and learning styles. For example, the following anchor activities may be used with Lesson 1 to help achieve English language proficiency standards.

Anchor Activities for Lesson 1

Starting Up	Beginning	Developing	Expanding	Bridging
Have students use worksheets to practice writing the names of the planets and other words from the vocabulary list.	Use the listening center with books on tape (multiple reading levels) about one of the planets. Draw a picture to show what was understood.	Search the Internet for information on the solar system and write a brief summary about what was understood.	Play a game like Clue that reveals certain details about the solar system. Details are hidden around the room. Students locate details and jot down notes.	Have students write reflection journals about what they learned and how they feel about space exploration.

Anchor activities may include extended content, related content, additional practice tasks, or a varied approach to applying information that students have already learned. Anchors can be designed for individuals to complete alone or be created for pairs or other small groups.

Anchor Activity Ideas
- Creating games or books
- Designing a PowerPoint presentation or using another form of multimedia that expands on a concept or topic covered
- Journal writing
- Learning or interest centers
- Accelerated reader
- Listening stations
- Activity box

Anchor activities work best when expectations are clear and the tasks are taught and practiced prior to use. Students must be held accountable for on-task behavior as well as task completion. Some benefits of anchor activities include using them to differentiate activities based on students' readiness, interest, intelligences, or learning styles; as a management strategy when working with small groups of students; and as a tool for making the class more student centered.

Differentiating Instruction with Kagan Structures

Kagan Structures are activities designed to produce thinking skills, communication skills, or mastery of high consensus content. There are over 150 Kagan Structures with different functions and purposes. A few favorite Kagan Structures are described in the following table.

Sample Kagan Structures

Kagan Structure	Description
Timed Pair Share	One student talks for specified time and the other listens. Then they switch roles.
Team Interview	Each student on a team in turn is interviewed by his or her teammates.
Numbered Heads Together	After the teacher asks a question, students write their own answer, discuss it in their groups, signal they are ready, and the teacher calls a number. Students with that number respond using a range of simultaneous response modes.
Boss/Secretary	One student ("Boss") dictates to another ("Secretary") who records the answer. The boss receives praise and then students switch roles.
Mix-N-Match	Students circulate in the room with cards, quizzing each other and then finding their match. For example, the person who has the picture of a shoe searches for the one who has the word *shoe*.

Source: Kagan, S., & High, J. (2002, Summer). "Sample Kagan Structures." *Kagan Online Magazine.* San Clemente, CA: Kagan Publishing. Reproduced with permission from Kagan Publishing. www.KaganOnline.com

The primary source for Kagan Structures is *Cooperative Learning* (Kagan, 1994), in which are found descriptions of well over 100 Kagan Structures, when to use them, and how to adapt them for use with English language learners. More Kagan Structures are described in *Multiple Intelligences: The Complete MI Book* (Kagan & Kagan, 1998), which presents simple methods to engage each of the eight intelligences. For example, with Kinesthetic Symbols, students learn to use their hands to symbolize content, engaging the bodily/kinesthetic intelligence. Those structures best suited for second language learning are described in *Second Language Learning through Cooperative Learning* (High, 1993), which also contains ready-to-use ESL activities to go along with the structures.

Guidelines for Managing a Differentiated Classroom

1. Have a behavior management plan in place. You must decide in advance how to respond to unanticipated events, such as a fire drill, an uncooperative student, students who need more time, and so on.

2. Teach students group and team skills. Give them opportunities to practice working in groups and centers.

3. Have available anchor activities for students when your attention is focused on an individual student. Anchor activities provide productive tasks for students to work on while you work directly with either a small group or one on one.

4. Sequence instructions in "chunks." Rather than giving long strings of directions, break them down into a small number of steps. Make sure that your expectations are clear.

5. Use time markers for differentiated tasks. Announce to students, "You'll have 10 minutes to work on this."

6. Let students know that there is an alternate plan for getting help when you are busy. For example, students can ask for help from a classmate who may share a similar language or be at a higher proficiency level.

Next you will want to consider *how* to manage a differentiated classroom. As you saw in the PowerPoint for brain-compatible differentiated instruction, sometimes teachers feel that a differentiated classroom requires extra work on their part. However, this does not have to be the case. Managing a differentiated classroom is very easily established and maintained with a few guidelines and suggestions.

Now that you are familiar with differentiating instruction, you will want to focus on planning purposely and effectively. Use the following tips to help you manage your planning process by deciding the before, during, and after steps for teaching a lesson:

Tips for Planning Lessons for English Language Learners

Before You Teach the Lesson

1. Determine the English language learning level of your ELLs. Be realistic about what you expect ELLs to do. (Identify what students know, understand, and what you want them to be able to do.)

2. Plan ahead. Think about how you will make the content comprehensible to your ELLs. Consider the following questions:
   - How will you link the content to the students' prior knowledge?
   - How will you build background information?
   - What language and content concepts need to be pretaught?
   - How will you develop critical content-area vocabulary?

3. Decide how you will accommodate multiple intelligences and learning styles.

4. Prepare or create visual aids such as maps, charts, pictures, and flashcards before the lesson is taught. Utilize multimedia wherever possible.

5. Create vocabulary word lists to accompany each lesson.

6. Adapt texts so that the concepts are paraphrased in English at multiple proficiency levels.

7. Search for nonfiction books in the library written at varying reader levels (graded readers) about the topic you are teaching.

During the Lesson

8. Build on what ELLs already know, including use of native language.
9. Simplify vocabulary and sentence structure. Preteach vocabulary in context.
10. Introduce concrete concepts and vocabulary first. (Refer to Marzano's site, www.infomarzanoandassociates.com)
11. Teach students to categorize their information using advance organizers or by semantic and story maps.
12. Demonstrate highlighting techniques to help students visually organize important information.
13. Review and repeat important concepts and vocabulary.
14. Provide concrete real-world examples and experiences.
15. Teach ELLs to use dictionaries to refine definitions for key vocabulary in the text.
16. Help ELLs become acquainted with their textbooks (table of contents, glossary, index, etc.).
17. Model thinking processes for students using think-alouds.

After the Lesson

18. When possible, have classmates make copies of their notes for ELLs to use.
19. Provide follow-up activities that reinforce language and content.
20. Have students work in small groups or pairs so that language and content are reinforced.
21. Plan homework assignments for ELLs according to their English language proficiency.
22. Create assessments that give your ELLs an opportunity to show what they have learned.

Meeting the Needs of English Language Learners

If you are a mainstream teacher or a beginning ESL teacher, you may never have experienced working with students whose language, background, and culture are different from your own. For some this can seem like an extra layer added to a pile of new duties that already face you. It is a challenging prospect to be faced with the responsibility of teaching a student or group of students with whom you are unable to fully communicate. This section will give you background information on some of the critical factors with which you should be familiar when working with English language learners.

Definition of English Language Learners

English language learner (ELL) is a term used to identify heterogeneous populations of students who share certain characteristics. As used here, the term refers to a person who has a first (home, primary, or native) language (L1) other than English and is in the process of learning and acquiring English. Many ELLs were born or have been living in the United States for many years in homes where family members and caregivers speak a language other than English. Even when English is their dominant language, they may not have developed oral and written language skills or the vocabulary necessary to function successfully at grade level in an English academic environment.

There are many acronyms associated with the education of English language learners, as the following list demonstrates.

Definitions of Terms Associated with English Language Learners

BSM	Bilingual Syntax Measure
CLD	Culturally and Linguistically Diverse
ELD	English Language Development
ELL	English Language Learner
ESL	English as a Second Language
FEP	Fluent English Proficient
LEP	Limited English Proficient
NABE	National Association for Bilingual Education
PPW	Pupil Personnel Worker
SDAIE	Specially Designed Academic Instruction in English
SLS	Speech Language Specialist
TESOL	Teachers of English to Speakers of Other Languages

Stages of Second Language Acquisition

Learning a second or additional language is a complex process. Second language acquisition is lengthy. Students move through five stages while developing English language proficiency:

1. *Preproduction.* Students observe and internalize the new language. They use nonverbal cues such as pointing and gesturing.
2. *Early production.* Students continue to acquire English and use language patterns such as yes/no responses and single words to communicate.
3. *Speech emergence.* Students begin to use simple sentences.
4. *Intermediate fluency.* Students are somewhat comfortable in social language situations. They state opinions and ask for clarification.
5. *Continued language development.* Students participate in classroom activities with support for comprehension.

Strategies for Helping English Language Learners

Once you are aware of and understand the stages of second language acquisition, it is also helpful to develop strategies for helping English language learners adjust to the school and your classroom.

Areas for Consideration	Plan of Action
Routines	Pair an ELL with a helpful student who shares the same L1 for the first few days.
School Schedules	Show the location of and explain the procedure for lunch, bathroom, dismissal, and so on. Visuals will help.
Supplies	Have a packet of supplies available for students until they can purchase items used by all students. Provide a list using illustrations or L1 text.
ESL Support	Arrange with the ESL teacher to schedule time for ESL support.
Student Comfort Level	Allow students to observe and absorb English without requiring production for a while. This will help relieve some of their anxiety.

As a classroom teacher with ELLs you must provide instruction that is meaning based, context rich, and cognitively demanding. An article on boosting academic achievement of ELLs in terms of literacy (American Educational Research Association, 2004) recommends the following components as part of reading instruction for these students:

1. Explicit instruction in word recognition through phonological awareness, practice reading, phonics, and frequent in-class assessments
2. Explicit instruction in skills that are needed to understand text, such as vocabulary building in context, strategies to aid comprehension, and help with academic oral language

ELLs are often placed in mainstream classes in which they are responsible for the same content as their English-speaking peers. The development of academic language proficiency takes from five to seven years for students learning a second language. While their monolingual peers continue to learn academic content, ELLs must develop both linguistic and cognitive skills in order to be successful.

Respect Newcomers' Silent Period

Be careful not to force newcomers to speak before they are ready. ELLs will acquire language when they have comprehensible input and their affective filter is low. Allow your students a "silent period" so they can acquire language by listening and trying to understand English.

Second Language
Acquisition

Check for Comprehension

Do comprehension checks frequently. If you ask, "Do you understand?" you will probably not get a reliable answer. Many students will answer "yes" when they do not understand. Make your questions more specific. Allow a response in the form of a drawing, pointing, gestures, or mime.

Building Bridges to Parental Involvement

Keep in mind that in some cultures parental involvement may not be a familiar practice. Work with your administrators and colleagues to devise ways to involve parents in your school and classroom.

Enhancing Literacy Skills for English Language Learners

ELLs do not need to be fluent in English in order to read and write in English. There are several successful approaches to building literacy skills. A reading/writing workshop approach allows ELLs to work at their own pace (see Lesson 7). With your guidance and instruction, ELLs will read and write at appropriate levels while participating in lessons, projects, activities, and group work with their peers. Remember, instruction often needs to be scaffolded for ELLs and teaching them reading and writing skills and strategies will be highly beneficial.

Students who are already literate in their home language (L1) learn to read at a higher level in English than those who are not. Literacy-related skills are transferred from one language to another even if the writing systems are quite different. Building L1 literacy is important. The importance of strong literacy skills is particularly evidenced in the *ESL Standards for Pre-K–12 Students*. For additional resources, view the following online PowerPoint presentations:

Collaborating to the Meet the Needs of ELLs
www.pdeinfo.state.pa.us/esl/lib/esl/Collaborating_Course_Part_III.April_15.ppt

Putting the Pieces Together to Meet the Needs of our ELLs
www.montgomeryschoolsmd.org/departments/cte/ppt/putting-pieces-together.ppt

No Child Left Behind

No Child Left
Behind

The No Child Left Behind Act (NCLB) of 2001 reauthorized the Elementary and Secondary Education Act (ESEA), the main federal law affecting education from kindergarten through high school. The passage of NCLB brings ELLs into the same context standards and accountability as their native English-speaking peers. These changes have major implications for mainstream teachers. In classrooms with diverse language populations, teachers must ensure that the curriculum and teaching strategies reflect alignment with English language proficiency standards. This context makes it imperative for schools to ensure that mainstream teachers gain a better understanding of the programs, theories, principles, and strategies that have proven successful in educating ELLs.

NCLB is built on four principles: accountability for results, more choices for parents, greater local control and flexibility, and an emphasis on doing what works based on scientific research. The tenets of NCLB are included in this book because they have direct impact on the schooling of ELLs. The impact of NCLB is directly related to instruction in ESL classrooms as well as mainstream classrooms with diverse language populations, as shown by the following aspects of NCLB:

- All ELLs must be tested at least once a year using an English proficiency test.
- ELLs who have been in U.S. schools for three consecutive years must be tested in reading/language arts using a test written in English, although students who meet certain criteria may receive a waiver for up to two more years.
- ELLs must meet specific annual targets of adequate yearly progress (AYP). Local and state education agencies will be held accountable for ensuring that ELLs meet these targets.

ESL Standards for Pre-K–12 Students and English Language Proficiency Standards

Brain-Compatible Differentiated Instruction for English Language Learners is aligned with *ESL Standards for Pre-K–12 Students* (2001), published by Teachers of English to Speakers of Other Languages (TESOL). The TESOL publication is organized around three overarching goals: the development of (1) social language, (2) academic language, and (3) sociocultural knowledge. Each goal supports three standards. Reaching these standards means that students demonstrate proficiency as English speakers, readers, and writers. The *ESL Standards for Pre-K–12 Students* is available to read or order online at www.tesol.org. (To read, click on Standards and Initiatives under Advancing the Profession of TESOL.) To order a copy, click on Publications and Products. In 2006 the national standards were abbreviated, making them more concise:

Standard 1. English language learners **communicate** for **social, intercultural, and instructional** purposes within the school setting.

Standard 2. English language learners **communicate** information, ideas, and concepts necessary for academic success in the area of **language arts.**

Standard 3. English language learners **communicate** information, ideas, and concepts necessary for academic success in the area of **mathematics.**

Standard 4. English language learners **communicate** information, ideas, and concepts necessary for academic success in the area of **science.**

Standard 5. English language learners **communicate** information, ideas, and concepts for academic success in the area of **social studies.**

Since many teachers are required to show evidence of standards-based teaching, this book will support documentation of standards-based planning as well as differentiating instruction to reach all English language learners. The following table demonstrates the TESOL *Pre-K–12 English Language Proficiency Standards.*

Proficiencies at Different Levels of English by Learners

Level 1 Starting	Level 2 Emerging	Level 3 Developing	Level 4 Expanding	Level 5 Bridging
Ability to understand and use—				
Language to communicate with others around basic concrete needs	Language to draw on simple and routine experiences to communicate with others	Language to communicate with others on familiar matters regularly encountered	Language in both concrete and abstract situations and ability to apply language to new experiences	A wide range of longer oral and written texts and increased recognition of implicit meanings
High-frequency words and memorized chunks of language	High-frequency and some general academic vocabulary and expressions	General and some specialized academic vocabulary and expressions	Specialized and some technical academic vocabulary and expressions	Technical academic vocabulary and expressions
Words, phrases, and chunks of language	Phrases or short sentences in oral or written communication	Expanded sentences in oral or written communication	A variety of sentence lengths of varying linguistic complexity in oral and written communication	A variety of sentence lengths of varying linguistic complexity in extended oral or written discourse
Pictorial, graphic, or nonverbal representations of language	Oral or written language, despite frequent errors that impede the meaning of the communication	Oral or written language despite errors that may impede the communication while retaining much of its meaning	Oral or written language with minimal errors that do not impede the overall meaning of the communication	Oral or written language approaching comparability to that of English-proficient peers

Source: TESOL. (2006). *Pre-K–12 English Language Proficiency Standards.* Alexandria, VA: Author. Copyright 2006 by Teachers of English to Speakers of Other Languages. Reproduced with permission of Teachers of English to Speakers of Other Languages via Copyright Clearance Center.

TESOL Performance Indicators and How to Read Them

Performance indicators are examples of observable, measurable language behaviors that English language learners can be expected to demonstrate as they engage in classroom tasks and approach the transition to the next level of English language proficiency. Performance indicators generally consist of three elements: content, language function, and support or strategy. Content indicates such information as, for example, parts of a microscope or artifacts or creatures of the past. Language function describes how students use language in communicating a message within a standard, such as the ability to identify from oral descriptions or to present and pose solutions. Support or strategy refers to ability to use and understand visual, graphic, or interactional methods related to the act of communication, such as pictures and illustrations or ability to interact in small groups or with a partner. Performance indicators, organized by standard and grade-level cluster, are interaction products of the five language proficiency levels.

Each performance indicator is read by grade clusters using grade level (1–3, 4–5, 6–8, and 9–12) and content area (language arts, math, science, and social studies).

The following is a sample of the performance indicators for grade level 6–8, Standard 2: English language learners **communicate** information, ideas, and concepts necessary for academic success in the area of language arts. The domains are the four skills of listening, speaking, reading, and writing; the topic describes what is being taught; and the five levels define the proficiency skills (TESOL, 2006).

Domain	Topic	Level 1	Level 2	Level 3	Level 4	Level 5
Listening	Synonyms Antonyms Metaphors Similes	Find words that are the same or opposite, represented by objects or illustrations according to oral directions	Match oral phrases involving figures of speech or vocabulary with visual representation	Identify figures of speech or vocabulary within visually supported oral discourse	Role-play scenes involving figures of speech or vocabulary based on oral descriptions	Respond nonverbally to demonstrate comprehension of figures of speech and vocabulary embedded in oral discourse
Speaking	Multiple meanings	Identify common words represented by objects or illustrations	Produce phrases or sentences with common words represented by objects or illustrations in two contexts	Give examples of words or phrases represented by objects or illustrations in multiple contexts	Explain differences in use of words or phrases with multiple meanings in varied contexts	Create and present scenarios that incorporate the use of words or phrases with multiple meanings
Reading	Comprehension strategies Technical texts	Match objects or diagrams with written labels with a partner to construct meaning	Use headings, bold print, diagrams, and charts with a partner to construct meaning	Use context clues within graphically and visually supported text with a partner to construct meaning	Use an array of strategies with visually supported text with a partner to infer meaning	Apply reading strategies to modified grade-level text to infer and validate meaning
Writing	Use of resources Editing Multimedia	Produce words or phrases using bilingual picture dictionaries	Check language structures, conventions, or spelling using computers, peers, or models	Peer-edit and revise drafts using checklists, models, or other resources	Self-edit and revise drafts using teacher feedback or other resources	Self-assess drafts and produce final products using rubrics, guides, or other resources

World-Class Instructional Design and Assessment (WIDA)

World-Class Instructional Design and Assessment (WIDA) CAN DO Descriptors are also performance indicators. WIDA is a consortium of states dedicated to the design and implementation of high standards and equitable educational opportunities for English language learners. The WIDA Consortium has developed English language proficiency standards and an English language proficiency test aligned with those standards (ACCESS for ELLs). Go to www.wida.us for more information. The consortium consists of eighteen partner states: Alabama, Delaware, the District of Columbia, Georgia, Illinois, Kentucky, Maine, New Hampshire, New Jersey, North Carolina, North Dakota, Oklahoma, Pennsylvania, Rhode Island, South Dakota, Vermont, Virginia, and Wisconsin. In the 2008–2009 school year, WIDA expected to serve about 700,000 ELLs in kindergarten through twelfth grade (WIDA, 2007/2008).

CAN DO Descriptors for WIDA's Levels of English Language Proficiency

Mainstream teachers or beginning teachers who may not be familiar with the English Language Proficiency Standards might want to use the CAN DO Descriptors as a useful tool for planning purposes. The CAN DO Descriptors widen the performance definitions by including indicators in each of the four skills domain areas: listening, speaking, reading, and writing. The usefulness of the Descriptors lies in the instructional language used and the easy access to planning differentiated lessons or unit plans. Another bonus to using the Descriptors is that they are sensory preferred and interactive through English Language Proficiency Level 4 (see Appendix I).

Second Language Acquisition Theory

A working understanding of second language acquisition theory is helpful for both ESL and mainstream teachers. Once you are equipped with this background knowledge, you will be better able to grasp the cognitive and linguistic stages ELLs experience. James Cummins postulated several important concepts related to second language acquisition (SLA) theory.

In 1983, Dr. Cummins introduced the acronyms BICS (basic interpersonal communication skills) and CALP (cognitive academic language proficiencies). According to Cummins, it should take ELLs at least two years to achieve BICS, enough English to communicate effectively in social situations, but at least five years to master CALP—sufficient academic skills to function effectively in English language classes with native speakers. He suggests that these two types of proficiency vary according to the degree of context available to the individual and the degree of cognitive challenge of the task. Content instruction offers a means by which ELL students can continue their academic or cognitive development while they are also acquiring academic language proficiency. The lessons provided in this book are basic ESL plans that concentrate on BICS and CALP.

In order to demonstrate these two types of language, Cummins created a quadrant model with questions ranging from cognitively undemanding/context embedded (e.g.,

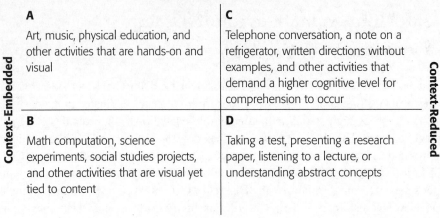

Cognitively Undemanding

	A	C
	Art, music, physical education, and other activities that are hands-on and visual	Telephone conversation, a note on a refrigerator, written directions without examples, and other activities that demand a higher cognitive level for comprehension to occur
	B	D
	Math computation, science experiments, social studies projects, and other activities that are visual yet tied to content	Taking a test, presenting a research paper, listening to a lecture, or understanding abstract concepts

Context-Embedded .... *Context-Reduced*

Cognitively Demanding

Source: Cummins, J. (2000). *Language, Power, and Pedagogy.* Clevedon, UK: Multilingual Matters. Reprinted by permission.

hold up a flower and ask students to point to the flower) to cognitively demanding/context reduced (e.g., ask students to write an essay telling how a flower grows). It is important that you practice moving students toward more demanding quadrants while retaining use of less demanding quadrants to consolidate gains—keeping the instruction grade-level appropriate and challenging, while differentiating and scaffolding. The quadrant model is demonstrated by the chart above.

There are numerous program models in second language education. Although two will be discussed in some depth, several others are in current use in North America, including the following:

- *50–50 Model.* Referred to as partial immersion in Canada, with academic instruction half a day in each language.
- *90–10 Model.* Referred to as early total immersion in Canada, with 90 percent of academic instruction is in the second language and 10 percent in the first language.
- *Bilingual Immersion Education.* Academic instruction given in both first and second languages for grades K–12.
- *Developmental Bilingual Education.* Academic instruction half a day in each language for grades K to 5 or 6. This used to be referred to as Maintenance Bilingual Education or Late Exit Bilingual Education.
- *English as a Second Language (ESL) or English to Speakers of Other Languages (ESOL).* All academic instruction in English.
- *ESL Content or Sheltered Instruction.* ESL Content classes are usually self-contained at the elementary level for one or two years, with a gradual shift to moving students to their age-appropriate grade-level classes. Secondary students attend classes taught by teachers with dual certification in ESL and a content-area subject.
- *ESL Pullout.* Students are taken out of the grade-level classroom for English language instruction according to grade level and language need. This method is the most expensive of all program models in bilingual/ESL education because it requires hiring extra resource teachers who are trained in second language acquisition (Chambers & Parrish, 1992; Crawford, 1997). In the United States, ESL pullout is the most implemented but least effective model (Thomas & Collier, 1997).
- *ESL Push-In.* Students can share the same native language or be from different language backgrounds. Students are given instruction in the mainstream classroom,

with the ESL teacher or instructional aide providing assistance, translation, or clarification.

- *Immersion.* Students attend specially designed content-area classes taught in the target language. Teachers are usually certified in both the content area and the target language.
- *Inclusion.* The ESL teacher and classroom teacher plan and teach together in the grade-level classroom.
- *Mainstreaming.* Once the ESL teacher determines that ESL students are proficient enough to move to all-English classes, the transition is made to content-centered courses.
- *Monitoring.* The ESL teacher monitors classroom progress of students who are close to exiting the ESL program as well as those students whose language needs are addressed in programs other than ESL.
- *Sheltered English.* This is a specialized form of an immersion program. Students coming from varying native language backgrounds are taught by a teacher with a background in both subject-matter and ESL pedagogy. Students usually have a regular ESL class as part of the curriculum.
- *Specially Designed Academic Instruction in English (SDAIE).* English is adapted to students' proficiency levels and supplemented by gestures, visual aids, manipulatives, and so on.
- *Structured English Immersion (SEI).* Only ELLs in class and preferably from one native language. All instruction is in English.
- *Submersion.* Students are "submerged" in regular content-area classes with no special second language instruction. Research indicates that students do not do well in this model and some schools elect to use a pullout model program to assist students.
- *Transitional Bilingual Education.* Academic instruction half a day in each language with gradual transition to all second language instruction in approximately two to three years.
- *Two-Way Bilingual Education.* Language majority and language minority students are taught together in the same bilingual class.

Program Models of Instruction

In this book, Lessons 1, 2, and 4 are sheltered (a means for making content comprehensible for ELLs while they are developing English proficiency) and Lessons 3 and 5 are content-based ESL (an instructional approach in which content topics are used as the vehicle for second language learning). Both are "on ramps" to building language!

Lesson 1	**Lesson 2**	**Lesson 3**	**Lesson 4**	**Lesson 5**
Sheltered Instruction (Pullout)	Sheltered Instruction (Push-In)	ESL Content with Sheltered Instruction	Sheltered Content	ESL Content

Lesson 6	**Lesson 7**
General Education ESL Inclusion	General Education Pullout

The SIOP Model of Sheltered Instruction

The Sheltered Instruction Observation Protocol is a research-based approach to sheltered instruction that has proven effective in addressing the needs of English language learners. The SIOP model was developed in a national research project conducted from 1996 to 2003, sponsored by the Center for Research on Education, Diversity and Excellence (CREDE). The model consists of eight components (CREDE, 2009):

1. Lesson preparation
2. Building background
3. Comprehensible input
4. Strategies
5. Interaction
6. Practice and application
7. Lesson delivery
8. Review and assessment

Using instructional strategies aligned with these components provides content-area teachers the appropriate tools to help ELLs develop academic English skills while learning grade-level content. The SIOP is also used as a model for lesson planning and implementation of high-quality sheltered instruction. In this book you will see how adaptations of the SIOP model components have been aligned with brain-compatible differentiated instruction.

Content-Based Instruction/Sheltered Instruction

How Languages
Are Learned
and Acquired

One teaching practice that draws on Stephen Krashen's theory of second language acquisition is integrated language and content instruction, or content-based learning. Krashen's emphasis that success in acquiring a second language depends on focusing on meaning rather than form, on language input being just slightly above the proficiency level of the learner, and in an environment that has ample opportunity for meaningful interaction fits well with the content-based learning approach, which provides conditions similar to those present in first language acquisition. This method of instruction is also known as Structured Immersion. In California it is known as Specially Designed Academic Instruction in English (SDAIE). This method of instruction requires significant teaching skills in both English language development and subject-specific instruction, clearly defined language and content objectives, modified curriculum, supplementary materials, and alternative assessments (Echevarria, Vogt, & Short, 2000).

Custodio and Sutton (1998) show how content-based instruction (CBI) could be used effectively in their own classrooms. Custodio, a middle school ESL teacher, used a *sheltered content model* for developing language with an introduction to U.S. history and culture. Students read historical fiction covering events from the explorations of Christopher Columbus to recent immigrations to the United States. Biographies, nonfiction, textbooks, drama, poetry, and multimedia supplement students' learning. Students enjoy many advantages from learning social studies through a variety of language materials: (a) oral and written language skills are developed in an integrated way, (b) students experience the past by imagining what life was like in different places and times, and (c) interdisciplinary activities such as map studies, timelines, art projects, music, and current events help establish connections within the sheltered content model.

Sutton, a high school ESL teacher, uses theme-based units focusing on young adult literature. Novels are selected relating to the students' cultures, based on varied reading levels, interests, and the degree to which the literature could connect with mainstream language arts classes. For example, one class read a novel, *Letters from Rifka,* about a Russian Jewish immigrant at the turn of the century. Then students learned literary terms, wrote about themes in the book, practiced journal writing and dictionary use, and had meaningful discussions about their own immigration experiences and compared them to those in the novel. The CBI approach in ESL classes can serve as a bridge to mainstream classes providing several important advantages such as (1) promoting higher-level thinking, (2) allowing for meaningful discussion of students' cultures as reflected in the literature, and (3) reinforcing thinking through manageable amounts of reading, writing, listening, and speaking skills.

Methods of Instruction

Two methods of instruction that align nicely with brain-compatible teaching are the Cognitive Academic Language Learning Approach (CALLA) and Total Physical Response (TPR). Both were designed to meet the needs of English learners.

Cognitive Academic Language Learning Approach (CALLA)

The CALLA instructional model was developed to meet the academic needs of students learning English as a second language in U.S. schools. The CALLA approach is targeted at ELLs at the advanced beginning and intermediate levels of English-language proficiency. Created to provide assistance for ELLs and thereby enable them to succeed in school with transitional instruction, CALLA was originally developed to meet the academic needs of three types of ELL students:

1. Students who have developed social communicative skills through beginning-level ESL classes or through exposure to an English-speaking environment but have not yet developed academic language skills appropriate to their grade level
2. Students who have acquired academic language skills in their native language and initial proficiency in English, but who need assistance in transferring concepts and skills learned in the first language to English
3. Bilingual English-dominant students who have not yet developed academic language skills in either language

The CALLA model has three components and instructional objectives in its curricular and instructional design: topics from the major content subjects, the development of academic language skills, and explicit instruction in learning strategies for both content and language acquisition. Teachers explicitly teach learning strategies at the same time that they develop language and content knowledge. The learning strategies therefore provide students with extra support for the negotiation of content-area instruction in the second language.

Chamot and O'Malley (1994, pp. 60–64) have identified three types of learning strategies:

1. Metacognitive Strategies
   - Advance organization
   - Organizational planning
   - Selective attention
   - Self-management
   - Monitoring comprehension
   - Monitoring production
   - Self-evaluation

2. Cognitive Strategies
   - Resourcing
   - Grouping
   - Note-taking
   - Elaboration of prior knowledge
   - Summarizing
   - Deduction/induction
   - Imagery
   - Auditory representation
   - Making inferences
3. Social/Affective Strategies
   - Questioning for clarification
   - Cooperation
   - Self-talk

Chamot and O'Malley recommend beginning CALLA lessons with ESL science, which provides many natural opportunities for hands-on discovery learning. ESL mathematics is next, because in the upper grades math is highly abstract and has a more restricted language register than science. Social studies is third, and English language arts is the fourth subject introduced because of the increasingly complex level of reading and writing required as well as the increase in underlying cultural assumptions (Chamot & O'Malley, 1994; O'Malley & Chamot, 1990). This method would work well in Lessons 1 and 4.

Total Physical Response

Total Physical Response (TPR), developed by James Asher, is based on the theory that second language acquisition is similar to a child's first language acquisition. That is, as a baby, our first involvement in language is through responding to commands our parents give us. Only after about one to two years do we begin, as toddlers, to produce comprehensible utterances in our first language. Reading and writing are introduced only after we have been speaking the language for an additional two to three years, as we enter school. According to Asher (1969), "Total Physical Response involves having students listen to a command in a foreign language and immediately respond with the appropriate physical action" (p. 4). TPR follows the premise that the human brain has a biological program for acquiring any language—including the sign language of the deaf.

Using TPR can be an effective brain-compatible approach to teaching ELLs. By design, TPR relies on movement (bodily/kinesthetic), listening (auditory), and watching (visual/spatial). TPR is an active learning approach for supporting comprehension in a low-anxiety atmosphere (Krashen & Terrell, 1983). For this reason, it is very popular with ELLs and teachers alike. TPR is also highly effective in teaching vocabulary associated with content-area knowledge. Teachers can introduce vocabulary and have students respond by drawing (visual/spatial), pointing (bodily/kinesthetic), putting pictures in order (logical/mathematical), or by any other physical response that utilizes active involvement and indicates comprehension.

General Principles of TPR

1. Listening comprehension develops before speaking.
2. Understanding should be developed through movements of the student's body.
3. Language learners should not be forced to speak. As students internalize language through listening comprehension, they will eventually reach a readiness to speak. An individual will spontaneously begin to produce spoken language.
4. TPR is a listening–speaking approach.

5. The teacher says each command and then models the action several times. The teacher gives the command and signals to students to perform the action.
6. A command is immediately followed by the corresponding action and body movement (Contiguity Principle).
7. Commands, grammatical structures, and vocabulary are repeatedly linked to their referent (Frequency Principle).
8. There is a cause-and-effect relationship between the uttered command and the action that follows (Feedback Principle).

Even in science and math students can gain a great deal of comprehensible input through the use of TPR (see Lessons 3 and 6). For example, any science experiment can be an opportunity to involve beginners through TPR. TPR also provides a base for literacy development in the second language as students learn to read the commands they have followed. The following box shows a sample TPR activity, in which ELLs work in teams of four to follow commands related to math skills.

The following sample of commands reviews and expands upon classroom procedures and introduces content language for a math class. The students easily understand the math in this sample and are learning the language for what they already know. TPR can also be used to teach new content, using the math vocabulary introduced in previous TPR activities to teach new concepts. However, whenever the concepts are new, they would be introduced first with math manipulatives prior to using numbers. In a TPR activity, only about seven of the words are new. It is important to review and build on the vocabulary learned previously. The new words are highlighted.

- Take out a piece of paper.
- Pick up your pen.
- Write your name on your paper in the upper right-hand corner.
- Write and **add** $2 + 4 =$ ____
- Raise your hand.
- Red team stand. Show us the answer with your fingers.
- Copy the **problem** $2 + 13 =$ ___.
- **Solve** the **problem.**
- **Check** the problem of the person next to you.
- Copy this **addition problem.**

$$\begin{array}{r} 25 \\ + 9 \\ \hline = \text{\_\_\_}. \end{array}$$

- First, **add** the numbers on the right.
- Write a 4 under the 9.
- Write the 1 above the 2.
- Add 1 and 2. Write 3 on the line in front of the 4.
- Count the numbers in the **problem.**
- Count the **digits** in each number.

- Look at the **addition problems** on the board.
- Blue team, go to the board and **solve** one **problem.**
- Students, **check** the answers.
- Yellow team, congratulate your teammate. Give your teammate a high-five.
- Everyone write one **addition problem** on your paper. Use only two numbers in your problem. Use one or two digits in your numbers. Pass the paper to the right.
- **Solve** the **problem.** Pass the paper to the right.
- Check the answer. Put your thumbs up if the answers are correct.

As students follow the commands, they are not asked to repeat. This reduces anxiety and enables attention to be focused on comprehension. Soon, however, several students will begin to repeat words, phrases, or sentences. As soon as some are comfortable saying the commands, they may begin giving similar directions to other students. The activities that preceded this one would have included fewer commands, shorter commands, and more limited vocabulary. When review is carefully incorporated into a sequence of TPR activities, complexity can increase quickly. Without this type of review, progress is very slow, and student retention is dramatically reduced.

Source: Gordon, J. (1996, Fall). "Using Total Physical Response to Teach Literacy to Intermediate and Secondary Students with Limited Literacy Skills." *Linguathon 2*(2). Reprinted by permission of the Illinois Resource Center.

Classroom Management

Your classroom should be regarded as a community. Within that community all members build relationships based on mutual respect. Daily routines and tasks are proactively planned so that classroom practices and teaching–learning structures promote acceptance of students from all cultural, social, and linguistic backgrounds (Balderrama & Díaz-Rico, 2006). Is there a difference between classroom management and classroom behavior/discipline? I think the answer is yes! In this section I describe the difference between *management* and *behavior/discipline* and give helpful suggestions for both the beginning and experienced teacher.

In my years of work as a teacher educator, I have witnessed teachers who need help managing their classrooms—forming groups, using centers effectively and creatively, handling students' papers, keeping track of homework assignments, creating seating arrangements, designing bulletin boards that are both instructive and constructive, managing large classes, and establishing daily routines. Additionally, they sometimes are clueless when it comes to handling behavior/discipline problems—responding when a fight erupts during class, working with an unwilling student who does not participate, handling a student who may exhibit signs of antisocial behavior, and confronting students who have problems sitting or concentrating for long periods of time.

When a teacher candidate goes for a job interview with either a building administrator or department chair, one of the first questions asked is "How do you describe your classroom management/discipline philosophy?" This is always a pertinent issue when hiring new teachers or even teachers with some classroom teaching experience—and rightfully so. Building administrators and department chairs want to be assured that a teacher entering the classroom has at least thought about and formulated a plan of action for managing a class. It is also reasonable to expect that the teacher candidate has had some practice either in field experience or student teacher internship with effective strategies for managing a classroom and for working with discipline issues that are probably going to occur at some point in time.

Working with English language learners adds another dimension to classroom management and behavior/discipline. Cultural and linguistic differences must be taken into account, considered, and embraced. Therefore, it becomes especially important for the teacher to have some background knowledge about each individual with whom she or he is working. This can be done by either conducting or requesting a profile on each learner. In Fairfax County, Virginia, it is called the "Intake Process" and on request this information can be made available to the classroom teacher. Learning about the cultures represented in your classes may explain some resistant or difficult behavior patterns. For instance, in some countries, students are schooled in single-sex classrooms. Often they are taught by same-sex teachers. Therefore, some boys may never have had female teachers just as some girls may never have had male teachers.

Demographic Changes—New Challenges and Opportunities!

Even if you do not know or understand the language and culture of your students, it is extremely important to know something about their backgrounds. For instance, it is helpful to have the following information on students:

- Student ability to speak, read, write, or understand their L1 and any other language(s)
- Parent/guardian ability to speak English and whether you can contact them for conferences or updates
- Religious considerations that may impact attendance and participation in certain activities
- Learning differences/disabilities (e.g., visual, auditory, physical)
- What the previous schooling was like, both formal and informal and any gaps in the student's schooling history (noting that prior academic schooling means different things depending on the country of origin; elementary or primary school may mean K–8, K–6, 1–6, or 1–5)
- Some background knowledge about how the student came to be in the United States, which can help teachers understand any psychological implications of a student's immigration status, such as refugee status immigrants who may be escaping violence, war, or political or religious persecution and whose responses to the effects of those issues may surface in the classroom

There are many facets of classroom management. Some of the most critical issues in classroom management will be discussed in the following sections.

Seating Arrangements

Depending on the size of your class and whether you are in your own room (as compared to sharing a room with another teacher), seating arrangements can be effective in helping students work individually or collaboratively. Chairs or tables can be arranged in groups, pairs, rows (theatre style), half circle, or square U, to name a few options. Smaller and younger children usually enjoy rug time for certain activities, while middle and high school students are typically more comfortable in chairs and desks arranged in a more traditional way. Again, consideration must be given to the fact that some ELLs may come from cultures in which classrooms consist of fifty or more students and rows of chairs and desks are the norm. What is most important in determining your seating arrangement is to make the learning environment optimal for the students. It may not always be convenient or possible to make a new seating arrangement (especially if you use another teacher's room). Therefore, you must plan to optimize your space regardless of the configuration.

Forming Groups

While moving students in a classroom may seem like a simple task, it can often lead to the teacher losing control and result in chaos. Therefore, the teacher needs to instruct and then model how to form groups. Depending on the age, level of proficiency, and space accommodations of the classroom, forming groups must be carefully thought out and orchestrated. This must be practiced with very clear and concise directions (spoken, use of symbols, written, or acted out). Some ideas for forming groups might include using cards with numbers, colors, symbols, animals, flowers, home country, language spoken at home, eye color, hair color, or shoe color.

To have students form groups of three, four, or five, have them choose strips of paper from a bag or basket and then move to the appropriate table or center based on the information on the paper. Label each table with the group's category title, such as

- Animal environments (desert, mountains, sea, jungle)
- Geographical areas (countries, continents, cities, states)
- Mathematical symbols $(+, -, \div, \times)$

Index Cards

Another easy way to have students form groups is to use index cards with stickers or pictures on them (depending on age and level of proficiency). For example, if you have a class of thirty students, make one stack of cards that puts students into six groups of five (red, blue, orange, green, yellow, and purple). Shuffle the cards and walk around the room and allow the student to choose a card. Let the students look at their cards, but not show or tell anyone. Then give directions for the activity. With practice and clear instructions, students should be able to get up and find their group. After their groups are formed, the teacher collects the cards for the next time.

Puzzle Pieces

Decide how many groups you want to make. Create a puzzle with the same number of pieces as students in a group. Glue a picture on a sheet of poster board and laminate. Cut the pieces apart and use a permanent marker to write the number of students in the group on the back of the pieces. Put these in plastic zip bags and when you are ready to use them give each student a puzzle piece. Then they must find the students with the rest of the puzzle. This works best if you use two or three shades of colored paper so if your class is large students will only look for their matching color.

Centers

Centers or learning stations are designated areas in the classroom intended for specific learning purposes. Designing centers that are effective and meaningful for ELLs is challenging because these students may not have a recognizable literacy level or the background knowledge (schema) to help them decode unfamiliar vocabulary words. Some ELLs may come from countries where cooperative learning or center instruction does not exist. As mentioned earlier, it is important to establish routines and practice them. When you practice, do not take anything for granted. Go through all the directions and expectations both orally, acting them out, and in writing, and always model what you want students to do.

If you wish to focus on students' literacy skills while enhancing listening, speaking, reading, and writing, developing centers can be a useful instructional tool. The following list provides some ideas for literacy centers:

- Listening Center
- Writing Center
- Word Study Center
- Poetry Center
- Reading Response Journals
- Independent/Buddy Reading

Bulletin Boards That Are Both Instructive and Constructive

Bulletin boards can be useful teaching tools that provide multiple paths to instruction for the classroom teacher. For instance, use the bulletin boards to create word walls. Change the boards according to themes or topics being covered. Post announcements, class rules and procedures, and student work. In an ESL classroom it is a good idea to have a flat paper map of the world. During the first week of school, have students identify their country of origin and then using push pins and yarn locate where your school is by stretching the yarn from each country represented along with the students' names. These boards can become quite attractive and students really take pride in bringing in their friends to show off the bulletin board. A perfect example is this book's cover photo!

Students' Papers

During the first week of school, assign everyone a chronological number. It is usually best just to go in alphabetical order in your grade book. Tell students that every time they turn in a paper the number should be in the right-hand corner of the paper. Once you have collected all the papers and put them in order, it is very easy to tell who did not turn in a paper. This works well and goes quickly.

Keeping Track of Homework Assignments—The IOU Book

Place a plain three-ring binder filled with blank spreadsheets in the room and tell students that this is the IOU Book. The spreadsheets are labeled with four columns: name, date, assignment, and a fourth column that the teacher initials when the assignment is completed. If students do not have their assignments, they must sign their names.

Managing Large Classes

Many teachers today are faced with large classes, ranging in sizes from twenty-five to forty. To a new or beginning ESL teacher, this can seem daunting. Along with large class sizes goes the likelihood of discipline problems or lack of student engagement, further complicated not only by the array of cultural and linguistic diversities but also by varying levels of cognitive abilities. Planning can be the key to smooth and seamless instruction. Remember to provide a variety of activities that include teacher-led, student-centered, pair, group, and individual self-paced work. Another approach is to create several small-group activities. Use mixed ability and language groups sometimes and designate a group leader with strengths to help weaker students. Try using same or similar-ability and same language groups to allow students to work at their own pace, thus permitting more challenging activities for stronger students and easier ones for weaker students.

Daily Routines

As mentioned throughout this book, establishing predictable routines is very important for effective classroom management. The classroom teacher is the bridge between students and what may be an unknown cultural setting and school system. Chances are very likely that your ELLs come from a culture with traditions and family values that differ from mainstream American culture. Every day these students are adjusting to new ways of saying and doing things.

When students enter the classroom each day they need to know what the expectations are and what procedures they are to follow. Students develop a sense of security and purpose when they know that the teacher has outlined in a clear and concise way what will take place. For instance, when students enter the classroom, try to have the day, date, warm-up activity, objectives, and homework written on the board or posted (a large tagboard or transparency for the overhead projector if you are not in your own classroom). It helps if these are in the same place every day. Beginning ELLs who may not speak any English will quickly learn by following the examples of others.

Students should be taught to enter the classroom quietly and in an orderly fashion. They should gather any materials that you have placed out (books, markers, notebooks, papers, or other materials). As shown in the lesson plan template, having objectives or an agenda available for students allows them to see the plan for the day and what the sequence of activities will be.

Depending on the length of time you have your students, it is important to be an astute observer in order to determine *how* students learn. This will influence how you acknowledge cultural differences and the amount of material that can be covered. Starting the day with a Morning Message, KWL (see Lessons 3 and 7), or similar activity is a good way to engage schema and serve as a point of departure for the day's lesson. Students should be given time markers throughout the lesson so they know and understand how much time they have on any given task.

Students must also be taught how to transition from one activity to the next. Practice, modeling, and clear instructions aid in making this successful. For instance, one teacher uses what she calls "musical motion" to move students from one activity to the next. When the students hear a certain song they know it is time to finish their work, clear their desks, and prepare to go to lunch or recess.

Similarly, at the end of the lesson, careful attention must be given to closure (see the lesson plan template). If homework is assigned, it must be reviewed and discussed to see whether there are questions and whether students understand what they are being asked to do. Do not assume that there will be someone at home who can help an ELL with homework. Closure may be a quick review of the day's lesson, having students write a reflection in their journals, playing a quick game to review learned information, or time given to start homework so the teacher can see whether there are questions.

Establishing Nonverbal Cues

Nonverbal cues in one culture may represent something entirely different in another. For instance, in Western cultures, when a student smiles at the teacher, it often indicates understanding. However, in many Asian cultures, smiling often disguises confusion or frustration. ELLs rely on both verbal and nonverbal cues. Beginning ELLs will need to watch your mouth when you speak as they are not only hearing the pronunciation of words but also watching as you form them with your lips and facial expression. These cues help provide meaning and aid in comprehension. Help students to link vocabulary to firsthand experiences with pictures, concrete objects, and real-life events. Model responses, encourage repetition, and foster routines in teacher–student and student–student interactions.

Beginning ELLs sometimes understand more English than they are able to produce orally. Try to find alternative ways for students to demonstrate their level of comprehension. For instance, if you are teaching a science unit (Lesson 4), have students put the picture parts on the microscope to demonstrate comprehension of the topic. Their ability to verbalize this comprehension will come later.

The following are a few suggestions for nonverbal cues:

- Ask the student to mime the action of what they are trying to convey.
- Have the student draw a picture of what they want to say.
- Pose questions that allow the student to respond with yes or no answers.
- Allow students to flip through pages in a book, pointing to specific pictures or letters.

Once these nonverbal cues have been established, it is important to use them consistently. In other words, students become accustomed to routines and they grow more comfortable with being risk takers when they can demonstrate comprehension in multiple ways.

Finally, educate yourself about your students' cultures. This will greatly help you to demonstrate that you value their heritage and it enables you to connect academic content to your students' experiences and background knowledge. Discipline issues can often be averted when both you and your students have a clear understanding about acceptable behavior and norms in both U.S. culture and those from which your students come.

Classroom Discipline

During the first week of school many teachers establish class rules. Sometimes these are created exclusively by the teacher; other teachers prefer to co-create these rules along with students. Sometimes rules are written as a discipline and consequence structure. It is easy to write rules that start with "Do not" or that say something is not permitted. Rules can be much more effective if presented in a positive way, such as "Listen when the teacher is talking" and "Come prepared to learn." Try to avoid using the word *not*. Also, limit your rules to about five. A lengthy list can become overwhelming and students may feel they can do nothing right. List only the rules you know you will enforce. If you are inconsistent in enforcing the rules, students will learn quickly that it is not important to follow them.

Students need to be taught skills, motivation, and attitudes that you want them to exhibit in order to eliminate or lessen discipline problems in the classroom. Once you have established your classroom rules, it is critical to stick with them and enforce them. Students will test the waters to see just what they can get away with and ELLs are no different. Check with your building administrators to determine the school or district policy about fighting, tardiness, disrespectful or foul language, and bullying.

Keep in mind that the bottom line for classroom behavior/discipline is to make every minute count. When students are engaged in the lesson and not bored, behavior/discipline issues are less likely to occur.

References

American Educational Research Association. (2004). English language learners: Boosting academic achievement. *Research Points: Essential Information for Education Policy, 2*(1). Washington, DC.

Asher, J. (1969). The Total Physical Response approach to second language learning. *The Modern Language Journal, 53*(1), 3–17.

Balderrama, M., & Díaz-Rico, L. (2006). *Teaching performance expectations for education of English learners.* Boston: Allyn & Bacon.

Center for Research on Education, Diversity, and Excellence (CREDE). (2009). *The sheltered instruction observation protocol.* Retrieved from http://crede.berkeley.edu

Chambers, J., & Parrish, T. (1992). *Meeting the challenge of language diversity: An evaluation of programs for pupils with limited proficiency in English.* Berkeley, CA: BW Associates.

Chamot, A. U., & O'Malley, M. (1994). *The CALLA handbook: Implementing the cognitive academic language learning approach.* New York: Longman.

Christison, M. (1996). Teaching and learning through multiple intelligences. *TESOL Journal, 46*(9), 10–14.

Cornett, C. (1983). *What you should know about teaching and learning styles.* Bloomington, IN: Phi Delta Kappa.

Crawford, J. (1997). *Best evidence: Research foundations of the Bilingual Education Act.* NCBE Report. Washington, DC: National Clearinghouse for Bilingual Education.

Cummins, J. (1983). Cognitive/academic language proficiency, linguistic interdependence, the optimum age question and some other matters. *Working Papers on Bilingualism,* No. 19, 121–129.

Cummins, J. (2000). *Language, power, and pedagogy.* Clevedon, UK: Multilingual Matters.

Custodio, B., & Sutton, M. J. (1998). Literature-based ESL for secondary school students. *TESOL Journal, 7*(5), 19–23.

De Avila, E., & Duncan, S. (1980). *Finding out/descubrimiento: Teacher's guide.* San Rafael, CA: Linguametrics Group.

Echevarria, J., Vogt, M. E., & Short, D. (2000). *Making content comprehensible for English language learners: The SIOP model.* Boston: Allyn & Bacon.

Ehrman, M., & Oxford, R. (1989). Effects of sex differences, career choice, and psychological type on adults' language learning strategies. *Modern Language Journal, 73*(1), 1–13.

Gahala, E., & Lange, D. (1997). Multiple intelligences: Multiple ways to help students learn foreign languages. *Northeast Conference on the Teaching of Foreign Languages Newsletter,* No. 41.

Gardner, H. (1983). *Frames of mind: The theory of multiple intelligences.* New York: Basic Books.

Glasgow, J. (1996). Let's plan it, map it, and show it! A dream vacation. *Journal of Adolescent and Adult Literacy, 40*(6), 456–467.

Glasgow, J., & Bush, M. (1996). Students use their multiple intelligences to develop promotional magazines for local businesses. *Journal of Adolescent and Adult Literacy, 39*(8), 638–649.

Gordon, J. (1996). Elementary example of total physical response: A strategy for beginning ELLs. Retrieved July 11, 2008, from Illinois Resource Center, www.dupage.k12.il.us/doc/3TOTAL%20PHYSICAL%RESPONSE.doc

Guild, P. (1997). Where do the learning theories overlap? *Educational Leadership, 55*(1), 30–31.

Haley, M. (2001). Understanding learner-centered instruction from the perspective of multiple intelligences. *Foreign Language Annals, 34*(4), 355–367.

Helmer, S., & Eddy, C. (2003). *Look at me when I talk to you: ESL learners in non-ESL classrooms.* Toronto: Pippin.

High, J. (1993). *Second language learning through cooperative learning.* San Clemente, CA: Kagan Publishing.

Kagan, S. (1994). *Cooperative learning.* San Clemente, CA: Kagan Publishing.

Kagan, S., & High, J. (2002, Summer). Kagan structures for English language learners. *Kagan Online Magazine.* Retrieved July 15, 2008, from www.cooperativelearning.com/KaganClub/FreeArticles/ASK17.html

Kagan, S., & Kagan, M. (1998). *Multiple intelligences: The complete MI book.* San Clemente, CA: Kagan Publishing.

Krashen, S., & Terrell, T. (1983). *The natural approach: Language acquisition in the classroom.* Oxford, UK: Pergamon Press.

O'Malley, M., & Chamot, A. U. (1990). *Learning strategies in second language acquisition.* Cambridge, UK: Cambridge University Press.

Oxford, R. (2003). *Learning styles and strategies: An overview* (pp. 1–25). Oxford, UK: Gala.

Teachers of English to Speakers of Other Languages (TESOL). (2006). *Pre-K–12 English language proficiency standards.* Alexandria, VA: Author.

Thomas, W., & Collier, V. (1997). *School effectiveness for language minority students.* Washington, DC: National Clearinghouse for Bilingual Education.

Tomlinson, C. (1999). *The differentiated classroom: Responding to the needs of all learners.* Alexandria, VA: Association for Supervision and Curriculum Development.

Tomlinson, C. (2000). Reconcilable differences? Standards-based teaching and differentiation. *Educational Leadership, 58*(1), 6–11.

World-Class Instructional Design and Assessment (WIDA) Consortium. (2007/2008). *WIDA CAN DO Descriptors.* Madison: Wisconsin Center for Education Research at the School of Education, University of Wisconsin.

SECTION TWO

Planning for Brain-Compatible Differentiated Instruction

One-Day Lessons

This book contains seven sample lessons. The seven lessons in Sections Two and Three are designed to demonstrate the impact and importance of careful planning for teaching both language and content. Teachers and researchers have worked collaboratively to create an effective approach to high-quality instruction for ELLs. The first five lessons are introduced as single-day plans but in fact may be taught over a period of time and can be easily adapted to fit most program models of instruction for English language learners. These plans will help you in getting started with planning instruction for ELLs. Begin by aligning your state and local standards to these plans and revise them so they work for you. Although the plans are written for one day, you may adjust them to meet your needs. You are encouraged to read each lesson and then use the template provided to re-create the plan to fit your own teaching circumstance. The planning grid is there to help you develop lessons that accommodate multiple intelligences and learning styles.

Remember, the PowerPoints are available for you when you feel you would like additional information or resources on the topics covered in the book. Also, note that words in bold are defined in the individual lesson glossaries. Finally, the reproducibles in Appendix M can easily be copied and modified to fit your needs.

Lesson 1

Visual Scaffolding through Content Science: The Solar System

PowerPoint

Scaffolding

Scaffolding is the term used to describe providing contextual supports for meaning through the use of simplified language, teacher modeling, visuals and graphics, cooperative learning, and hands-on learning (Ovando, Collier, & Combs, 2003, p. 345). If you teach ELLs you must provide that support. As students become more proficient, the scaffold is gradually removed (Díaz-Rico & Weed, 2002, p. 85).

According to Bradley and Bradley (2004), three types of scaffolding have been identified as being especially effective for ELLs:

- *Simplifying the language.*   The teacher can simplify the language by shortening selections, speaking in the present tense, and avoiding the use of idioms.
- *Asking for completion, not generation.*   The teacher can have students choose answers from a list or complete a partially finished outline or paragraph.
- *Using visuals.*   The teacher can present information and ask students to respond through the use of graphic organizers, tables, charts, outlines, and graphs.

While there are many types of scaffolding, this lesson focuses on using visuals in a science lesson.

Science presents a unique opportunity to combine rich language learning with hands-on experiential knowledge acquisition. The visual and tangible nature of scientific exploration allows students of differing levels of language proficiency to truly grasp concepts without the pressure of linguistic perfection. "Science gives a rich context for genuine language use. From a language acquisition perspective, science can serve as a focal point around which oral language and literacy in ESL can develop" (Reilly, 1988, p. 273). It is essential to make science an interactive area of learning in order to reach out to ELLs and give them a comfortable platform from which to construct new understanding of ideas as well as build **academic language.**

Before You Begin

It would be helpful to display images and materials in the classroom about space and the solar system. This should include a center or area of the room with many theme-related books and posters. You will want to create planet picture cards. Use index cards to glue pictures of the planets on one set and descriptions on the other set. Have the vocabulary for this lesson on a word wall. Students should copy the vocabulary and definitions using notebooks or index cards that can be laminated. If you have a computer in the classroom, open the browser to a theme-related page. This bit of preparation will help inspire interest and give students the feeling that they are actively exploring as they learn.

Scenario

Miss Burke is a fourth-grade ESL teacher whose school uses a pullout program model. T~~h~~ class consists of twenty students from varying linguistic backgrounds. Though two students extremely limited conversational ability in English, they are literate in their native lang~~uage~~ have some prior knowledge of the subject. Four students are at a beginning prof~~iciency~~ and the remainder range from starting up to expanding. This is day three in stud~~ying the solar~~ system and the planets.

Brain-compatible learning

Standards and Intelligences

TESOL Standards

STANDARD 4 • English language learners **communicate** information, ideas, and concepts necessary for academic success in the area of **science.**

GOAL 2, STANDARD 1 • To use English to achieve academically in all content areas: Students will use English to interact in the classroom.

GOAL 2, STANDARD 3 • Students will use appropriate learning strategies to construct and apply academic knowledge.

Virginia Standards of Learning: Science 4.7

www.doe.Virginia.gov/VDOE/Superintendent/Sols/science4.pdf

No Child Left Behind

Craft lessons to make sure each student meets or exceeds the standards.

Intelligences and Learning Styles Accommodated

| Bodily/ Kinesthetic | Auditory | Logical/ Mathematical | Interpersonal/ Social |

| Intrapersonal/ Introspective | Visual/ Spatial | Verbal/ Linguistic |

Planning Phase

Objectives

1. **Content:** Students will be able to name, describe, and order the planets.
2. **Language:** Students will be able to write descriptions of the planets.

Materials

- Index cards with solar system pictures and descriptions
- Photocopies of reproducible pages for students
- Books, posters, charts, and other solar system realia
- Large cut-outs of the solar system placed on the walls or floor
- Black construction paper and colored chalk

Vocabulary

Planets • Solar system

–––––––––––––––––––– Teaching Phase ––––––––––––––––––––

Warm-Up

This lesson can begin with a quick review of the solar system using the large cut-outs. They can be displayed on the wall or on the floor in an open space. Start by naming the planets, moon, and sun. Ask for volunteers to share some fact that they learned from days one and two. Utilize the word wall and allow students to use their vocabulary list copied in their notebooks or index cards. Show students the PowerPoint on the solar system found at www.rockingham.k12.Va.US/resources/elementary/4science.htm#7powerpoints

Transition

Ask students to use the books and materials in the classroom to go on a five-minute tour of space. Allow students to take this time to explore the resources you have placed in the room. Then create a living solar system by placing students in order around a student acting as the sun. Show them how the planets revolve by moving them and for higher proficiency level students, mark the floor using tape to show and explain to them the impact of seasonal changes.

Activity 1: The Living Solar System

Give each student a card with either a planet name or picture for a partner match. Have students match up with their partner so each picture has a name with it. Review matches with students. Have students line up in the order they think the planets are in. Put the sun at the front of the line.

Activity 2: Discovering the Marvels of Space

Have students return to their seats and view *The Solar System*, available at http://unitedstreaming .com. Remind students to remember who their partner is because they will be working again with that person after the video. Show the first twelve minutes of the video and pay careful attention to students' reactions (to determine level of comprehension). Higher-level students can take notes on new pieces of information learned. Then have students get back with their partners and tell them that they are going to search for more information about the solar system by using the books and resources provided in the classroom. They are to spend fifteen to twenty minutes reading about the planet on their card and look for its size, position, age, and makeup (composition). This vocabulary has already been pretaught but a quick review is always helpful. Have students use the graphic organizer provided to list this information. For the four beginning-level students, either use picture books or search for books or materials in their native language.

Activity 3: Partners Share Information

Since there will be at least ten pairs to share, have students report their findings on their worksheets. Later they will work on writing more descriptive sentences from their readings. You may have a large posterboard with the planets listed on it. Have students take turns filling in the information as it is reported.

Differentiating Instruction

Starting Up.   Students at this level can participate easily in Activity 1 as it is visual and kinesthetic, requiring less linguistic interaction. Name the planets in the solar system. (Activity 1)

Beginning.   Students can benefit from listening and mirroring the words and actions of other students while learning the ideas in their own ways. Describe the planets in the solar system. (Activity 1)

Developing.   Students can use visual cues to guide their understanding and use of the academic language. Identify features of the moon or sun. They can apply this learning to their participation. (Activity 2)

Expanding.   Students will be able to act as leaders in the third activity, guiding others and demonstrating understanding of concepts and words. Discuss and give an example and description of a star in the solar system. (Activity 3)

Bridging.   Students may use the list of optional activities and choose one to work on. Explain the relationships between the planets and the solar system. (Activity 3)

Assessment

Informal assessment of student comprehension for this lesson can be observational as each student takes part in both whole-group and paired activities. Keep records of the students' responses and interaction as they are learning. The closing activity can also serve as a test of knowledge gained during the lesson.

Closure

Ask students to use black paper and colored chalk to draw their own depiction of the solar system. Here you are looking to remind them about each planet and its special characteristics discussed earlier to see if they can take that knowledge and apply it to their drawings. In this way, you have the opportunity to observe and assess comprehension. See the reproducible activity titled "Solar System Checklist."

Conclusion

The activities in this lesson are designed to continue study of the solar system as well as give the students a functional understanding of names, description, and order. Notice how the plan moves the teaching from teacher centered to whole class to paired work and then to the individual. This engages students and allows for observation and work with less proficient students. Pullout program models often require the ESL teacher to work with students from multiple mainstream classes. Therefore, you will need to understand how to manage and move students with little distraction. Since the class has such a variety of proficiency levels, there are numerous activities that tap into the learning styles and intelligences of all learners.

Homework

Have books on the solar system available from the library in your classroom. Allow students to take these home to help in completing the homework worksheet. For students who are at higher proficiency levels and have Internet access, they may use online resources or select from the optional list of activities. Beginning and lower-level students may draw pictures to show what they have learned and/or complete the reproducible activity titled "Solar System Activity."

———————— WHAT IF Factors ————————

1. What if you have a bridging-level student who knows a great deal about the solar system and wants to share what he or she knows? Because it may be too much information for your other students, have this student select two or three activities from the options list and designate a day and time to present to the class.
2. What if you feel that some students are not grasping the academic language associated with the topic? Move around to the paired activities and ask questions as comprehension checks. This way you can interact with the students to determine where there may be gaps.

— Optional Brain-Compatible Activities for This Lesson —

Students gather information about a planet or moon at Astronomy for Kids (www.astronomy.com/content/static/AstroForKids) and create a Kid Pix movie. Have them read and record their own descriptions.

Have students collect data online at http://kids.nineplanets.com and make their own spreadsheets and charts comparing the diameters of planets, as well as comparisons of gravity, temperature, distance from the sun, and composition.

Have students create short claymation movies illustrating the rotation and revolution cycles of the planets. Sudents will need non-drying clay, a web-cam, and Windows Movie Maker.

 Play a recording of *The Planets Suite* by Gustav Holst and have students try to interpret the music for each planet using a jazz chant, interpretive dance, drawings, or poetry.

 Have students use the computer to locate FunBrain games (www.funbrain.com).

FunSchool (www.funschool.com) also has space games for upper-level students.

Teacher's Reflection

"The lesson worked very well with this group of twenty students. Since my school uses the pullout model, the students in this class come from five mainstream classes. What worked particularly well was having a nice variety of activities. Fourth graders like it when we change activities and this lesson accommodated visual, auditory, and kinesthetic learners. The advanced-level learners really liked the optional activities since they all have technology skills. This lesson gave me several opportunities to do comprehension checks to ensure that both content and language objectives were met and that students engaged in all four skills: listening, speaking, reading, and writing."

Theory to Practice

Using systematic visual or semantic graphs regarding the content of a social studies or science passage facilitates memory and content area achievement (Report of the National Reading Panel, 2000).

Lesson 1   Performance Indicator   Standard 4 • Grade Level 4–5

Domain	Topic	Level 1	Level 2	Level 3	Level 4	Level 5
Speaking	The solar system	Name the planets in the solar system	Describe the planets in the solar system	Identify features of the moon or sun	Discuss and give examples of stars in the solar system	Explain relationships among the planets of the solar system

Glossary of Terms

academic language Words and ideas integral to comprehension of content-area concepts.

Reproducible Activities

Now It's Your Turn!

Reflect and then respond to the following:

1. Write two facts or ideas you learned from the lesson.
2. Write one question you would like to have answered about the lesson.
3. Indicate how you would teach the lesson differently.
4. What are some ways you can get students to connect ideas in science?

Questions for Discussion

1. How can the teacher make this lesson more lively and interactive for the two students who have limited English and may be new arrivals?
2. In what way can this teacher provide additional support activities for the mainstream teachers from whose classes these students are pulled out?

3. What manipulatives might the teacher use in working with students who are graphically and visually talented?

References

Bradley, K., & Bradley, J. (2004, May). Scaffolding academic learning for second language learners. *The Internet TESL Journal, X*(5). Retrieved July 14, 2008, from http://iteslj.org

Díaz-Rico, L., & Weed, K. Z. (2002). *The crosscultural, language, and academic development handbook: A complete K–12 reference guide* (2nd ed.). Boston: Allyn & Bacon.

Discovery Education (2007). *The solar system* [video file]. Retrieved March 15, 2007, from http://unitedstreaming.com

National Reading Panel. (2000). *Teaching children to read.* Jessup, MD: National Institute for Literacy at EDPubs.

Ovando, C., Collier, V., & Combs, M. (2003). *Bilingual and ESL classrooms: Teaching multicultural contexts* (3rd ed.). Boston: McGraw-Hill.

Reilly, T. (1988). *ESL through Content Area Instruction.* Washington, DC: ERIC Clearinghouse on Languages and Linguistics. (ED 296 572)

Lesson 2 Dialogic Approach to Building Vocabulary in Content Social Studies: Economics and Interdependence

Building vocabulary is of primary importance in working with English language learners. You can make difficult reading comprehensible by building vocabulary, decoding difficult syntax, and teaching background knowledge. Researchers Beck, McKeown, and Kucan (2008) recommend choosing vocabulary words by determining their usefulness, frequency, and the ease with which students can restate the meaning in their own words. They distinguish three types of vocabulary words:

- Tier 1 words are basic words that need to be taught, such as *baby, clock,* and *jump.*
- Tier 2 words are words that a student will see frequently but are difficult enough that special instruction is needed, such as *fortunate, maintain,* and *coincidence.*
- Tier 3 words occur infrequently and are mostly specific to certain content areas, such as *lathe, refinery,* and *isotope.*

Students can keep track of vocabulary words in various ways, including vocabulary notebooks or on index cards that they hold together with rubber bands or ring clips. You may also have students create vocabulary question cards (student-generated vocabulary questions) or word-within-a-word cards (highlighting prefixes and suffixes).

Economics seems like a daunting topic to explore with elementary students, especially English language learners. However, the concepts that guide economics can be applied to real-life situations and are of great use to students in their everyday lives as they negotiate cultural meanings and norms. "Without economics instruction during their elementary school years, these students are not likely to acquire the knowledge and skills necessary for functioning successfully within the American economic system" (Laney, 1993). Movement and images are proven ways of helping ELLs absorb and internalize meaning. The following activities in this lesson are designed to build basic economic understanding as well as tangible concept connections to everyday life.

Before You Begin

In order to facilitate this lesson, it is essential to know your students and consider ways to make the ideas accessible to all learners. In this situation, where ELL and native English-speaking students are combined, peer mentoring is a great benefit to learners. You will need to provide oral language prompts and model vocabulary throughout the lesson. Working in collaboration with the ESL teacher provides an excellent resource and support. A rich environment that surrounds students with the content will enhance ELLs' entire learning experience. The classroom setting should include books, posters, DVDs, word walls, diagrams, and student work, which all help support vocabulary building.

Scenario

Ms. Bailey is a third-grade classroom teacher whose class consists of twenty-eight students, ten of whom are English language learners. Ms. Gill is the ESL teacher who goes into the classroom to team teach with Miss Bailey (**push-in model**). In order to ensure that all students are learning the same information, the teachers plan social studies lessons together, allowing for differentiation and accommodations for linguistic diversity. This is day five in studying this topic and students have already learned basic vocabulary about goods and services.

—————————— Standards and Intelligences ——————————

TESOL Standards

STANDARD 5 • English language learners **communicate** information, ideas, and concepts for academic success in the area of **social studies.**

GOAL 1, STANDARD 3 • To use English to communicate in social settings: Students will use learning strategies to extend their communicative competence.

GOAL 2, STANDARD 2 • To use English to achieve academically in all content areas: Students will use English to obtain, process, construct, and provide subject matter information in spoken and written form.

Virginia Standards of Learning: Economics 3.8

www.doe.Virginia.gov/go/Sols/history3.pdf

No Child Left Behind

Reduce the gaps in achievement among students from diverse backgrounds.

Intelligences and Learning Styles Accommodated

| Bodily/ | Auditory | Musical/ | Logical/ |
| Kinesthetic | | Rhythmic | Mathematical |

| Interpersonal/ | Visual/ | Verbal/ |
| Social | Spatial | Linguistic |

—————————— Planning Phase ——————————

Objectives

1. **Content:** Students will be able to identify aspects of **interdependence,** as it pertains to careers.
2. **Language:** Students will be able to draw conclusions both orally and in writing about how one person's job or work affects others and other people's jobs.

Materials

- Batteries, unsharpened pencil, paper, pencil sharpener, index cards
- Poster paper
- Dry erase boards
- Picture dictionaries
- Flashcards

Vocabulary

Careers and jobs • Interdependence

Teaching Phase

Warm-Up

Use the United Streaming video site (http://unitedstreamingvideo.com) to watch *A Career for Buster.* Ask students to jot down the names of the careers mentioned in the video. Have beginning-level ELLs put a check mark next to the careers mentioned that they can identify. See Careers and Interdependence Worksheet. Discuss what students wrote.

Transition

Have four students go to the front of the classroom. Give one student batteries, one student an unsharpened pencil, one a sheet of paper, and the fourth student a pencil sharpener (that runs on batteries). Tell them they need to use their items to work together and write the names of three careers, products, and services. Then allow the students to say what they need to do to be able to write. (Put the batteries in the pencil sharpener and sharpen the pencil and then write on the paper.) Ask them what would happen if the student with the pencil wasn't there. Discuss the ways they depend on each other. Ms. Bailey and Ms. Gill model this activity with one of them trying to write on the board *without* chalk or marker. They discuss how one is dependent on the other to provide chalk or a marker.

Activity 1

Assign each student a career by giving them an index card with a job name on it. Explain that they must talk to other students in the room to find out if they need each other in some way to do their jobs. As they find others on whom they depend, ask them to write the name of that job on the back of their index card. (Having these connections written down is a good way for students to review the idea of interdependence later.) At the end of ten minutes, ask students to find the other person or people they rely on the most in their job. Teachers may need to assist in placing students in pairs or groups of three if they are unsure of where they fit in best.

Ms. Gill may allow beginning-level ELLs to use their L1 while working with this group to reinforce vocabulary using the word wall, picture dictionaries, or flashcards.

Here is a list of careers that work well for this activity:

police officer	bus driver	car mechanic
farmer	waiter/waitress	construction worker
banker	pilot	chef
computer expert	artist	author
accountant	book publisher	teacher
athlete	doctor	shoemaker
rock star	car salesperson	

Activity 2: Numbered Heads Together

Count off students from 1 to 4. Call out a question: "What does a teacher depend on?" Students in teams put their heads together to discuss the answer. They must make sure everyone on the team knows the answer. Randomly call a number from 1 to 4 (use a spinner, draw popsicle sticks out of a cup, roll a die, etc.). The student whose number is called writes the answer on a dry erase board or piece of paper. When all teams are ready, have the designated student stand and hold up their response to show their answer. Check each team's answer for accuracy. Repeat with additional questions as time permits.

Activity 3

Distribute the worksheet titled "Interdependence Chains." Have a copy of this either on the overhead projector or on a large piece of poster paper. The teachers model this first. Using their books, vocabulary notebooks, and other resources available in the room, this activity is to be completed collaboratively. Check for comprehension through observation. Developing, expanding, and bridging ELLs should be expected to produce language that uses higher-order thinking skills and a wider range of vocabulary expressions.

Differentiating Instruction

Starting Up.   Differentiate for these students by giving them words with pictures to accompany them. If you have many students at this level, it would be a good idea to have pictures on all of the job cards. Identify jobs or careers from pictures. (Activity 1)

Beginning.   Scaffold instruction for these students if they need to use L1 and L2. Match pictures with a corresponding artifact or symbol. They may also work as starting up students. (Activity 1)

Developing.   Have students create vocabulary question cards with answers and word-within-a-word cards. Place artifacts presented in oral presentation in pairs according to their interdependence. (Activity 1)

Expanding.   Create scenes using the vocabulary based on a video or movie. (Activity 3)

Bridging.   Use the Economics Review Sheet to create a skit or musical presentation (a commercial jingle or jazz chant). Interpret videos, movies, or oral readings about jobs/careers and interdependence. (Activity 2)

Assessment

On a table at the front of the room, place items that are related to careers (e.g., a stethoscope, toy airplane, book, toy tractor, police badge, paint brush, or hammer). Have students select as many items as they can identify and write conclusions they can draw about how one person's job or work affects other people's jobs. Create a rubric that assesses identification and the conclusions drawn.

Closure

Students can draw posters or pictures to represent the interdependent relationships they have discovered during the activity. These can be posted in an area of the room dedicated to Interdependence and used for later review.

Conclusion

This lesson will get students to begin to think in terms of how businesses and people rely on each other to function. It is a springboard for later discussions of supply and demand as well as a connection to other cultural studies of interdependence to include bartering systems. By posting the ideas and student-drawn interpretations of interdependent relationships in the classroom, you can create a setting that will encourage use of that knowledge in later lessons.

Homework

Interview your parents. What are their jobs? How do their jobs depend on others? Who depends on them? Use the interdependence chain to show what you learn. Students may use their L1 for these interviews.

WHAT IF Factors

1. What if you have a student with **attention deficit disorder** (ADD) who is having trouble focusing on the task? Provide this student with steps or stages of performance that can be checked off as they are completed.
2. What if students find a connection between two jobs that is not clear? Help students to "unpack" the language. Ask the students to try to explain the connection and their ideas while other students ask them questions. This can become a useful conversational exercise as well as a way to further examine the concept of interdependence.

Teacher's Reflection

"I especially like the push-in model because it's having two teachers in the classroom. Ms. Gill and I plan every day and her knowledge about ELLs is invaluable to me. I don't hesitate to ask questions and knowing more about second language acquisition helps me better understand what my ELLs are experiencing."

Theory to Practice

Teachers can plan activities that vary by speaking level. At the beginning stage, when the goal is fluency, students can work in homogeneous groups (Balderrama & Díaz-Rico, 2006).

Lesson 2   Performance Indicator   Standard 5 • Grade Level 1–3

Domain	Topic	Level 1	Level 2	Level 3	Level 4	Level 5
Listening	Interdependence of jobs/careers	Identify jobs/careers from pictures	Match pictures of jobs/careers with a corresponding artifact or symbol	Place artifacts presented in oral presentation in pairs according to their interdependence	Create scenes using the vocabulary based on a video or movie	Interpret videos, movies, or oral readings about jobs/careers and interdependence

Glossary of Terms

attention deficit disorder A persistent pattern of inattention and hyperactivity, impulsivity, or both, occurring more frequently and severely than is typical in individuals at a comparable level of development.

interdependence The way in which people, professions, or businesses depend on each other in order to do their jobs or effectively function.

push-in model Program model in which the ESL teacher goes into the mainstream general educator's classroom and works with ELLs.

Reproducible Activities

Now It's Your Turn!

Reflect and then respond to the following:

1. Use the lesson plan grid found in Appendix A and rewrite the lesson for a high school (grades 9–10) mainstream inclusion class with seven ELLs of varying proficiency levels.
2. Create an assessment activity that scaffolds content for the ELLs.
3. Stories are a great way to get students interested in a topic that may otherwise seem uninteresting. Create a story or identify a fable or folktale that you can use to introduce students to economics and interdependence.
4. How might you use multimedia to further expand this lesson?

Questions for Discussion

1. In a push-in program model, the ESL teacher sometimes is made to feel like an instructional assistant. What steps can be taken to insure that both teachers' roles are equally important to the educational process?
2. What are some possible accommodations for students with learning differences that also provide instruction in both content and language?
3. How can you as a teacher include students' cultural backgrounds when discussing jobs or careers?

References

Balderrama, M., & Díaz-Rico, L. (2006). *Teaching performance expectations for educating English learners.* Boston: Allyn & Bacon.

Beck, I., McKeown, M., & Kucan, L. (2008). *Creating robust vocabulary.* New York: Guilford Publications.

Discovery Education. (2007). *A career for Buster* [video file]. Retrieved March 15, 2007, from http://unitedstreaming.com

Laney, James D. (1993). Economics for elementary school students: Research-supported principles of teaching and learning that guide classroom practice (electronic version). *Social Studies, 84*(3), 99–103.

Lesson 3   Building Comprehension Using Graphic Organizers—Content Science: Plant and Animal Cells

Second Language Aquisition

Graphic organizers are one way to stimulate nonlinguistic thinking (Marzano, 2004). Graphic organizers allow students who have difficulty expressing themselves in writing the option of drawing pictures. These pictures are important because they represent the connection between prior and new knowledge they have constructed. Graphic organizers can be used both as activities and assessments. Peregoy and Boyle (2005) state that meaningful lessons need to be **scaffolded** while still being challenging (**i + 1**). Graphic organizers provide teachers a way to break down these challenging concepts so that they are more meaningful and can lower a student's **affective filter.** Additionally, they can be used to accommodate those students who learn better with visual representations (Haley, 2000).

Using graphic organizers helps students with cognitively demanding work by representing thinking visually. Students are able to analyze, connect, relate, and contrast ideas and concepts. In classes where much of the content is covered orally, the addition of graphic organizers helps ELLs to better organize information. Similarly, graphic organizers can help ELLs demonstrate their comprehension of more complex ideas that they may not be capable of explaining well in English.

Graphic organizers such as concept maps, timelines, flow charts, and T-charts provide students with visual tools to organize, understand, and remember vocabulary concepts and key ideas. By teaching students how to use graphic organizers, students can record information while reading or listening. You must remember to provide scaffolding for students as they begin to use graphic organizers by filling in some of the information beforehand. As students gain more proficiency, you can gradually remove the scaffold by filling in less and less information. Eventually, the students will be able to independently organize information.

Before You Begin

You will need to cut out and glue questions onto note cards. To ensure durability, you can print on cardstock and laminate the cards. Additionally, if you think it is helpful, allow students to use a bilingual dictionary during instruction since many scientific words are difficult to understand. You should also make copies of each worksheet on an overhead for students who are visual learners and need additional support. The Word Chart reproducible in this lesson can be used in many different forms. Students can work in pairs or in groups. You decide its use depending on the proficiency level of each student. Each level of thinking in this organizer is intended to increase students' understanding of their target word. Allow students to help each other to promote a more collaborative classroom atmosphere, particularly during the exploration of cells part of this lesson.

Scenario

Ms. Rodriguez is a seventh-grade ESL teacher who teaches an ESL content class with **sheltered instruction.** There are thirty students—fourteen boys and sixteen girls. Nine children are native

Spanish speakers; other languages include Farsi, Korean, Thai, and Hmong. The science class is ninety minutes long. The Spanish-speaking students vary in proficiency levels, ranging from beginning to expanding. The Farsi-speaking student is more advanced in both verbal and written skills. There are two students with identified special needs and both have experienced an interruption in schooling. This is day two for this topic.

Standards and Intelligences

TESOL Standards

STANDARD 4 • English language learners **communicate** information, ideas, and concepts necessary for academic success in the area of **science.**

GOAL 1, STANDARD 3 • To use English in social settings: Students will use learning strategies to extend their communicative competence.

GOAL 2, STANDARD 1 • To use English to achieve academically in all content areas: Students will use English to interact in the classroom.

GOAL 2, STANDARD 2 • To use English to achieve academically in all content areas: Students will use English to obtain, process, construct, and provide subject matter information in spoken and written form.

Virginia Standards of Learning: Life Science LS.2

www.doe.Virginia.gov/go/Sols/sciencsesol.pdf

No Child Left Behind

Provide maximum opportunities for children to read at grade level.

Intelligences and Learning Styles Accommodated

| Bodily/ Kinesthetic | Verbal/ Linguistic | Interpersonal/ Social | Visual/ Spatial | Auditory |

Planning Phase

Objectives

1. **Language:** Students will be able to complete a word chart graphic organizer for one new vocabulary word related to the lesson.
2. **Language:** Students will be able to describe in writing or orally at least one of the major components of a cell, including cell wall, cell membrane, and nucleus.
3. **Content:** Students will be able to compare and contrast what an animal cell and a plant cell look like, their functions, and their main differences in structure using a Venn diagram graphic organizer.

Materials

- Note cards
- Graphic organizers
- Science text
- Word chart

- Colored markers
- Microscopes
- Cell slides

Vocabulary

Animal cell   •   Plant cell

---------------------- **Teaching Phase** ----------------------

Warm-Up

Show students pictures of a plant and animal cell already labeled. Ask them, "How are they the same?" "How are they different?" Compare their responses by writing them on a T-Chart on the overhead projector. Encourage students to use their vocabulary list. Starting up students and beginning students may have difficulty with the language in this lesson. These students can practice copying the vocabulary list into their binders.

Transition

Students will use **KWL** charts to review new vocabulary words learned. Students write what they know; what they want to know; and what they learned after reading. Students will each be assigned one "Word of the Day" accompanied with a Word Chart graphic organizer (see Reproducibles). This graphic organizer gives students an opportunity to use a new vocabulary word and add words to describe it throughout class. The Word Chart should be finished by the end of class. Starting up students and beginning students can use visuals taken from science textbooks or selected online pictures to begin connecting a printed vocabulary word with a visual/tactile item.

Activity 1

Students will continue to activate their prior knowledge about cells. Give them one question precut and glued to a note card. Students will write their answers to these questions on the numbered tagboards taped along the wall (see Reproducibles). You then assess each question after the responses are posted. As a cooperative strategy, have students listen to and practice their oral skills while sharing their responses with the class.

Activity 2

Students will do a shared reading to learn about an animal and a plant cell in their textbook, *Life Science* (Glencoe-McGraw Hill, 2000, pp. 43–44 and excerpts from pp. 45–52). If possible, pair starting up students and beginning students with a partner whose L1 is the same. If this is not feasible, the teacher should model the steps with these learners, using bodily/kinesthetic motions to actively engage learners. Also, having them repeat the vocabulary as they are looking through the microscope will aid comprehension. Pictures of two types of cells will be highlighted: animal cells and plant cells. Transparencies of both cells will be on the overhead throughout the reading to help show the differences as new information is discovered. Students will discuss the major differences between each cell and follow directions for the mini lab on animal and plant cells (see Reproducibles). Additional textbooks that could be used instead include *Glencoe Science* (Glencoe-McGraw Hill, 2000), *Harcourt Science* (Harcourt School, 2000), *Science Explorer* (Prentice Hall, 2002), and *Scott Foresman Science* (Addison-Wesley, 2000).

Differentiating Instruction

Starting Up. Students can draw pictures for the warm-up. Students can work with a partner so the mini lab procedures can be modeled. Have students match descriptive words to pictures. (Activity 1)

Beginning. Students can classify short descriptions using the graphic organizers to help their understanding of the procedures for the lab. After using the book to copy the cell pictures, students can identify similarities of cells. (Activity 2)

Developing. Students can sort information visually and graphically by identifying some similarities and differences between the cells. They can also expand their knowledge by reading about cell division and growth. (Activity 2)

Expanding. Students can identify the functions of parts of a cell and can describe sequential steps of photosynthesis. (Activities 1 and 2)

Bridging. Students can conduct an experiment designed to engage in critical thinking and to make predictions (e.g., examining and comparing cells of domestic animals to those of animals used in research for curing common diseases). Expanding and bridging students should also be asked to make inferences and predictions about how cells live in plants and animals. (Activities 1 and 2)

Assessment

Students will discuss what the **Venn diagram** graphic organizer is and as a class fill in one example on the animal cells side and one example on the plant cells side. Allow for time to complete two more entries in the Venn diagram. Go around and check students' answers and ask for the students' help with filling in the similarities they observed. The teachers should have a completed Venn diagram to use as a model. This works best on a posterboard or on the overhead projector. Starting up students and beginning students may work collaboratively to complete this task and use of L1 is permissible. To scaffold the diagram for beginners, an unlined diagram can be printed out for the student to draw pictures. Assessment will be informal, based on classroom participation, teacher feedback on warm-up, and the mini lab. Try to give feedback throughout the class. The Venn diagram should be revisited in the next class. Higher proficiency level students can be given the assessment titled "Comparing Plant and Animal Cells—Assessment" (see Reproducibles).

Closure

Have students read their "Word of the Day" from their word charts. They will share their descriptive words. More students will share the next class. To bring closure try doing a ball toss to one student to orally summarize animal or plant cells, their functions, and components while the transparencies are on the overhead. Once they have answered, they toss the ball to another student. You may also wish to use a wonderful PowerPoint on cells located at www.alleghany .k12.va.us/DGB_ITRT/PP%20Presentations/Science.

Conclusion

Graphic organizers are useful tools that enable students to organize thoughts in a meaningful way, thus helping them to recall information. This lesson highlighted a few of the more typical and useful graphic organizers. Students are introduced to differences and similarities between an animal and a plant cell. Students will be able to describe the function of the major components of a cell and will have multiple opportunities for observing, recording, drawing, and analyzing data in their journals to demonstrate comprehension.

Homework

Students can start this homework in class. Students should choose either the "Drawing a Plant Cell" or the "Drawing an Animal Cell" worksheet for homework (see Reproducibles).They will label their pictures. Students may use books to refer back to the reading shared in classes. Students with a lower proficiency level will color or draw a picture of the cell of their choice and label what they can. Higher proficiency students can begin a project that includes making a model of a plant or animal cell. Instructions for this project or others can be found at www .scienceproject.com.

————————————————— **WHAT IF Factor** —————————————————

What if students are not familiar with using graphic organizers? Graphic organizers are most commonly used for content courses and can break down difficult concepts. However, the number of graphic organizers available on the Internet and in books can be overwhelming. You can put graphic organizers in a binder organized by units or labeled by the organizer name to keep a variety of differentiated organizers readily available. Additionally, if lower proficiency students have difficulty with the science labs, you can have varying graphic organizers available to aid in comprehension. Allow beginners to work with a partner who speaks their first language. Ensure that enough wait time is provided for every proficiency level, especially when students are introduced to new vocabulary.

—— Additional Resources for Plant and Animal Cells ——

- www.teach-nology.com/worksheets/science/cell
  Provides plant and animal cell worksheets, puzzle makers, biology labs, and related resources.

- www.lessonplanet.com
  Offers lesson plans and worksheets that are aligned with state standards and hands-on and interactive activities for all grade levels. Search for "plant and animal cells" to find specific activities for this lesson.

- www.school.discoveryeducation.com/lessonplans/activities/electronmicroscope
  Provides students with a virtual lesson on how to use a microscope. Included are thorough explanations of the differences between plant and animal cells.

- www.education-world.com/a_lesson/02/lp259-05.shtml
  Provides a wealth of information, including lesson plans, instructions for making three-dimensional models of plant and animal cells, assessment tools for all grade levels, activities that are aligned with state standards, and articles on how to creatively engage students while studying this topic.

—— Teacher's Reflection ——

"Even though this lesson is fun to teach, it takes a great deal of prior preparation. The microscopes have to be carefully placed out for students and then put back on the mobile cart for the next teacher. Another challenge is providing enough scaffolding for beginning-level students while coming up with challenging projects for the more advanced-level students."

—— Theory to Practice ——

Graphic organizers, probably the most widely used bridge to visualization, provide an alternative to the traditional outlining and note-taking of ideas (Ogle, 2000).

Lesson 3   Performance Indicator   Standard 4 • Grade Level 6–8

Domain	Topic	Level 1	Level 2	Level 3	Level 4	Level 5
Reading	Plant and animal cells	Match descriptive phrases or words to diagrams or models	Classify short descriptions using visual or graphic organizers	Find or sort visually or graphically information about plant and or animal cells	Transform graphically supported expository text into sequenced steps to illustrate processes	Make predictions or inferences (e.g., consequences) from modified grade-level material

Glossary of Terms

affective filter Affective variables such as motivation, self-confidence, and anxiety. When students feel comfortable being risk takers in the learning environment, their affective filters are lowered.

graphic organizers Visual representations that help organize information or facts.

i + 1 Students receive second language input that is one step beyond their current stage of linguistic competence. For example, if a learner is at a stage "i," then acquisition takes place when he or she is exposed to "comprehensible input" from level "i + 1."

KWL Instructional technique that allows teachers to activate students' prior knowledge by asking them what they already **K**now; students then set goals specifying what they **W**ant to learn; and after reading, students discuss what they have **L**earned.

scaffold Providing contextual supports for meaning through the use of simplified language, visuals and graphics, and hands-on experiences.

sheltered instruction A content subject (math, science, social studies) taught to ELLs by a teacher who has certification in the content area being taught as well as specialized training in instructional strategies designed to meet linguistic and cultural needs.

Venn diagram An illustration used to show similarities and/or differences between sets (groups of things).

Reproducible Activities

Now It's Your Turn!

Reflect and then respond to the following:

1. What are your experiences with using graphic organizers? How have they been useful (or not)?
2. Describe ways to lower students' affective filters.
3. Create a different warm-up and closure activity for the lesson.
4. Give an example of how to use i + 1 with students in this class for each of the proficiency levels.

Questions for Discussion

1. What are some ways the teacher may lower students' affective filters in order for them to be more willing risk takers?
2. What are some ways that curriculum intended for older learners can be used effectively as a supplement for teaching grade-level content concepts? Give examples.
3. Identify other types of appropriate scaffolding for this lesson that allow students to successfully access content and language objectives.

References

Haley, M. H. (2000, November/December). Refocusing the lens: A closer look at culturally and linguistically diverse exceptional students. *ESL Magazine, 3*(6), 14–16.

Marzano, R. J. (2004). *Building on background knowledge for academic achievement: Research on what works in schools.* Alexandria, VA: Association for Supervision and Curriculum Development.

Ogle, D. M. (2000). Make it visual: A picture is worth a thousand words. In M. McLaughlin & M. Vogt (Eds.), *Creativity and innovation in content area teaching.* Norwood, MA: Christopher-Gordon.

Peregoy, S. F., & Boyle, O. F. (2005). *Reading, writing, and learning in ESL* (3rd ed.). Boston: Pearson Education.

Lesson 4   Vocabulary Processing in Content Science: Using Interactive Notebooks to Learn about Microscopes

Interactive notebooks enable learning as an interactive process (Teachers' Curriculum Institute, 1999). Working with ELLs *requires* an interactive approach, particularly in content-based classes. Teachers need to develop and activate background knowledge, deliver content that is contextualized, and use **realia** to make input comprehensible (Haley & Austin, 2004). Interactive notebooks allow students to use several types of writing and innovative graphic techniques to record their work, becoming portfolios of individual learning. Students have multiple ways to process ideas, and they are encouraged to use critical thinking and be more creative, independent thinkers.

Graphic organizers are **visual scaffolds** used to help activate prior knowledge and organize new information. **Comprehensible input** and **output** are essential to acquiring a second language. Graphic organizers provide the *input* and can be glued onto the right side of a spiral notebook, while what was learned, or the *output,* can be processed on the left side of the notebook. The input and output set-up of this interactive notebook encourage students to reflect on, or *interact* with, and ultimately process new information. The right side of the notebook is used for teacher input. On the left side students demonstrate their understanding of the information being learned. Students are encouraged to be imaginative and creative and to utilize their multiple intelligences and learning styles.

Metacognition results from students' experiences and reflections. This process builds the bridge between prior knowledge and new knowledge (Haley & Austin, 2004). Graphic organizers and interactive notebooks help ELLs learn and process a new language, while simultaneously providing you with an opportunity to informally assess your students. Students can select their best medium to explore and learn new content. ELLs can draw pictures of what they learned if they do not have written language.

Before You Begin

You will need a large amount of appropriate materials at graded levels within the classroom to promote narrow reading. Krashen (as cited in Peregoy & Boyle, 2005) encourages narrow reading, in which students read multiple texts about the content, in this case, microscopes and cells. According to Krashen (as cited in Peregoy & Boyle, 2005), narrow reading helps build vocabulary *and* background knowledge. You can collaborate with other science teachers and the librarians for support with books and supplementary materials. In addition to creating a literature-rich environment, you should also download the United Streaming video clips beforehand to avoid possible streaming problems or other technical difficulties during the lesson.

Scenario

Ms. Rosario is an eighth-grade ESL teacher whose class is an ESL content class with **sheltered instruction.** There are thirty-two students—twenty-five boys and seven girls, some of whom have experienced an interruption in their education. All of the children are native Spanish speakers. The science class is fifty minutes long. All of the students range from beginning to expanding.

Two students, however, are still in their silent period. This is the first day for this topic. The following days will include experiments that require measuring, analyzing, and collecting data.

Standards and Intelligences

TESOL Standards

STANDARD 4 • English language learners **communicate** information, ideas, and concepts necessary for academic success in the area of **science.**

GOAL 2, STANDARD 1 • To use English to achieve academically in all content areas: Students will use English to interact in the classroom.

GOAL 2, STANDARD 3 • Students will use appropriate learning strategies to construct and apply academic knowledge.

GOAL 3, STANDARD 1 • To use English in socially and culturally appropriate ways: Students will use the appropriate language according to audience, purpose, and setting to communicate with peers in the classroom.

Virginia Standards of Learning: Chemistry CH.1

www.doe.Virginia.gov/VDOE/Superintendent/Sols/sciencsechemistry.pdf

No Child Left Behind

Provide children with an enriched educational program that increases the amount and quality of instructional time. Diversity, equity, and collaborative behavior are also supported among all students.

Intelligences and Learning Styles Accommodated

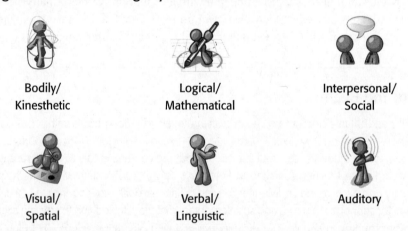

| Bodily/ Kinesthetic | Logical/ Mathematical | Interpersonal/ Social |
| Visual/ Spatial | Verbal/ Linguistic | Auditory |

Planning Phase

Objectives

1. **Content:** Students will be able to identify and label at least two parts of the microscope.
2. **Language:** Students will be able to orally demonstrate the parts and the safe and appropriate use of a microscope.

Materials

- Microscopes
- Video
- Interactive notebooks

Vocabulary

Microscope parts

Teaching Phase

Warm-Up

To tap into prior knowledge, students will share what they *Know* about microscopes on their KWL graphic organizer (see Reproducibles). Students will orally share while student responses are written on the overhead. Students will glue their KWLs on the right side of their interactive notebooks.

Transition

Identifying what students *Want* to learn on a KWL chart can be challenging, especially for beginners, so you should provide some background information about microscopes. Students will turn to Chapter 2, "Cells: The Units of Life," in the *Life Science* book and do a shared reading of pages 40 to 43 (Daniel, Ortleb, & Biggs, 2000). The passage is about what a compound microscope is used for and the history of how microscopes have evolved. Students will identify whether there is anything they *Want* to learn about microscopes. You then transition into the first activity by telling the students that they will now learn how to hold a microscope and identify some of its parts.

Activity 1: How to Use a Microscope Properly

Students will learn how to properly use a compound microscope. They will complete a cloze activity (Activity 1 in the Reproducibles) while viewing a one-minute-and-fifty-one-second clip from United Streaming, *Procedures for Using a Compound Microscope* (Discovery Education, 2007). You may wish to create an optional worksheet for students with little or no English. Have them draw what they learned from the video instead of doing the cloze passage. Students will have an opportunity to practice labeling a microscope properly after the cloze activity.

Activity 2: Parts of the Microscope

These vocabulary words can be cut out and attached with Velcro to the posterboard picture of the microscope. You identify and point to the parts of the microscope. A poster of a microscope with blank spaces will be in the front of the classroom. Students will repeat the name of the parts aloud while they attach the Velcro words from a plastic baggie to their laminated sheets of the microscope (see Reproducibles).

Differentiating Instruction

Starting Up.   The video and projector serve as visual aids. Students with a visual impairment should be seated closer to the teacher and the overhead to allow for constant comprehension checks. Students will practice holding the microscope properly. (Activity 1)

Beginning.   Students can draw pictures about what they learned and read along with the cloze passage. Have students write the parts of the microscope. (Activity 1)

Developing.   Students will highlight and read the words in the cloze activity and may be able to help beginners hold the microscope properly. Have students compare parts of the microscope using information from multiple sources. (Activity 1)

Expanding.   Students can fill in the blanks in the cloze passage and can hold a microscope while identifying at least two parts. Have students narrate the personal impact of the use of a microscope. (Activity 1)

Bridging.   Students can match several parts in front of the class and be able to name their functions. Have students interpret the global impact the microscope has had as a scientific tool. (Activity 2)

Assessment

Students will write down two new words they learned this day on the left side of their notebooks. Throughout class, the teacher will informally assess students on the matching exercise to determine comprehension and on oral responses or drawings on their KWL charts. Allow students additional wait time, particularly with the introduction of new vocabulary. Students will engage in self-assessment while the cloze passage is read aloud. Higher proficiency students can be assessed on their ability to identify parts and functions as well as an interpretation of the global impact of the microscope.

Closure

You should review vocabulary words and reinforce them by pointing to the microscope parts. Students will be asked to list what they *Learned* about the microscope on their KWL charts.

Students will turn in their KWL charts as an exit pass which will serve as an informal assessment. In order to get ready for the next class, students will return the microscope correctly back to the appropriate place (also an informal assessment).

Conclusion

Interactive notebooks allow students to use multiple intelligences and learning styles. Students can use many types of writing and graphic techniques. These notebooks allow students to draw or write what they learned about microscopes. Some of the many benefits of using interactive notebooks include helping students to organize information, sequencing assignments, providing opportunities to spiral instruction, and encouraging pride in student work.

Homework

Students will complete a matching worksheet labeled with parts of the microscope (see Reproducibles). The functions of each part are listed next to the word. Higher proficiency students will also create a three-sentence cloze activity with the vocabulary words in a word bank to share with the class the next day.

—————————————— WHAT IF Factor ——————————————

What if a student has been absent for an extended period of time? Such a case would serve as a good opportunity for students to teach someone who missed the original presentation. Students would read the daily agenda book and review what had been done each day. The teacher should provide copies of any missed handouts.

— Optional Brain-Compatible Resources for This Lesson —

- http://bugscope.beckman.uiuc.edu
  Bugscope enables students to access images from a scanning electron microscope via the Internet. The site also has a gallery of images to view and resources for teachers.
- www.ou.edu/research/electron/www-vl/long.shtml
  The World Wide Web Virtual Library microscopy page has hundreds of links to sites devoted to microscopy, images, education, and more.
- http://sciencespot.net
  The Science Spot website has worksheets, activities, and games about microscopes and many other scientific concepts.
- www.mos.org/sln/sem/intro.html
  Boston's Museum of Science hosts a webpage devoted to the scanning electron microscope.
- www.pbrc.hawaii.edu/bemf/microangela
  MicroAngela features numerous scanning electron microscope (SEM) images.
- www.uq.edu.au/nanoworld
  Nanoworld, from the Centre for Microscopy and Microanalysis at the University of Queensland, provides even more SEM images.

--- **Teacher's Reflection** ---

"Since school equipment like microscopes is expensive, I have learned to proceed slowly with this topic. It usually takes one full period just to introduce the microscope and assess for comprehension on its appropriate use. The ELLs in the class move quickly with this information as much of it is hands-on and visual. Since this is only day one, I can quickly determine if they have understood the content. The more advanced proficiency level students enjoy having the chance to explore other kinds of microscopes as they read through the grade-level books I provide for them."

--- **Theory to Practice** ---

Simulations increase meaning, are highly motivating, and facilitate transfer of knowledge (Wolfe, 2001).

Lesson 4   Performance Indicator   Standard 4 • Grade Level 6–8

Domain	Topic	Level 1	Level 2	Level 3	Level 4	Level 5
Writing	Microscopes	Draw and label charts or features of the microscope	Describe features of the microscope	Compare features of the microscope using information from multiple sources	Narrate personal impact of use of a microscope	Interpret global impact microscope has had as a scientific tool

Glossary of Terms

comprehensible input Purposeful language used by the teacher so that it is meaningful to the learner.

comprehensible output Language produced by a language learner that represents an understanding of content.

graphic organizers Visual organization of information to aid comprehension.

metacognition The knowledge of one's own thinking and learning.

realia Real-life objects and materials used for instructional purposes.

visual scaffolds Temporary visual support materials that aid language comprehension for beginning language learners.

Reproducible Activities

Vocabulary List—Lesson 4   166
KWL Chart: Microscopes   167
Activity 1: Procedures for Using a Compound
    Microscope   168
Activity 2: Label the Microscope   169

Now It's Your Turn!

Reflect and then respond to the following:

1. Create an interactive notebook according to the description given at the beginning of the lesson. Indicate which intelligences and learning styles are accommodated.
2. Using the planning grid found in Appendix A write a lesson plan for day two on this topic.

3. Use the optional brain-compatible resources listed in this lesson to create a portfolio of images that will be useful for expanding the focus of the content.

4. If you do not have a science or chemistry background, what steps will you take to learn more about this topic?

Questions for Discussion

1. Discuss the importance of teachers modeling activities for students. How can this be done in a multisensory way so that multiple intelligences and learning styles are accommodated?

2. Create a list of steps that you feel are important to follow when giving instructions to students. For instance, is it effective to say directions over and over again? If not, how can you avoid this and be certain that you've effectively explained the task you are asking learners to complete?

3. Identify two to three enrichment activities that you can create to accompany this lesson. These should be activities to have on hand in the event that some students finish early or need to have a multimodal approach to this topic. When should you use these?

References

Daniel, L., Ortleb, E., & Biggs, A. (2000). *Life science.* Chicago: McGraw-Hill/Glencoe.

Discovery Education. (2007). *Procedures for using a compound microscope* [video file]. Retrieved March 15, 2007, from http://unitedstreaming.com

Haley, M., & Austin, T. (2004). *Content-based second language teaching and learning: An interactive approach.* Boston: Allyn & Bacon.

Peregoy, S. F., & Boyle, O. F. (2005). *Reading, writing and learning in ESL: A resource book for K–12 teachers* (3rd ed.). New York: Addison Wesley Longman.

Teachers' Curriculum Institute. (1999). *History alive: Interactive student notebook.* Palo Alto, CA: Author.

Wolfe, P. (2001). *Brain matters: Translating research into classroom practice.* Alexandria, VA: Association for Supervision and Curriculum Development.

Lesson 5 *Improving Literacy Instruction in Language Arts: Using a Directed Reading–Thinking Activity*

A **directed reading–thinking activity (DRTA)** helps boost reading comprehension by helping students understand how proficient readers make predictions as they read (Stauffer, 1970). Teachers guide students through the prediction process until they are able to do it on their own by asking students to make predictions and then reading to confirm their ideas (Balderrama & Díaz-Rico, 2006). Using reciprocal teaching, students predict, summarize, ask questions, and suspend judgment, using these techniques with one another (Palinscar & Brown, 1984). DRTA also provides a flexible social learning setting in which teachers can design complementary activities that easily accommodate a variety of reading levels, intelligences, and learning styles. General use of this strategy involves small-group instruction for reading text from any genre. The text is selected by the teacher, who acts as a careful observer of reading behavior (Visser & Hanggi, 1999).

The procedures for a DRTA are simple and straightforward:

1. Students read selection title (and maybe the first two to four pages) and make predictions about the content.
2. Students read to the first predetermined stop. They confirm, refine, or reject their initial hypotheses, justifying their ideas with reference to the text. They can then make new hypotheses.
3. Students read the next section and follow the procedures in step two above. This process continues until the entire selection is read.
4. Follow-up activities may be completed after the text is read.

Before You Begin

Be aware that you will have learners who may have varying degrees of literacy in both their first and second language. While **reading strategies** such as DRTA are beneficial for all levels of language learners, it is essential to **scaffold** instruction in the activities to meet individual students' needs.

Prior to this lesson you will have taught folktales and other genres listed on the vocabulary list. For this lesson you must present background information on *realistic fiction:* books that are set in the present day, in which characters encounter modern-day difficulties and dilemmas. Realistic fiction includes mysteries, adventure stories, humorous stories, such as *The Magic Bed* (Burningham, 2003), and much more. Since a form of technology is used, a CD player, make sure that the equipment is working and set to go before class begins.

Scenario

Ms. Chu is a ninth-grade ESL English teacher whose class consists of thirty-two students. The ELL students are native speakers of either Mandarin Chinese or Korean. The students' levels of proficiency range from developing to bridging. English classes are seventy-five minutes long on block scheduling. This class meets five times per week. They are in day five on this topic.

--------- **Standards and Intelligences** ---------

TESOL Standards

STANDARD 2 • English language learners **communicate** information, ideas, and concepts necessary for academic success in the area of **language arts.**

GOAL 1, STANDARD 2 • To use English in social settings: Students will interact in, through, and with spoken and written English for personal expression and enjoyment.

GOAL 2, STANDARD 1 • To use English to achieve academically in all content areas: Students will use English to interact in the classroom.

Virginia Standards of Learning: English 9.3

www.doe.Virginia.gov/VDOE/Superintendents/Sols/2002/EnglishSecondary.pdf

No Child Left Behind

Promote a climate that supports equity, diversity, and collaborative behavior.

Intelligences [ ] ed

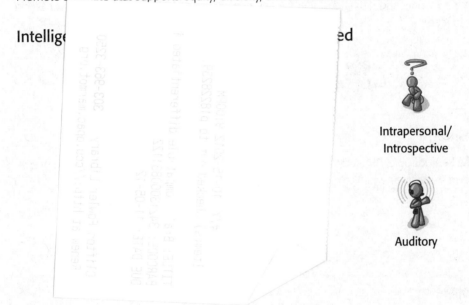

Intrapersonal/ Introspective

Auditory

--------- **Planning Phase** ---------

Objectives

1. **Content:** Students will be able to identify and discuss differences between realistic fiction, folktales, and other literary genres.
2. **Content:** Students will be able to identify and discuss literary elements of realistic fiction.
3. **Language:** Students will be able to summarize the components of their alarm bed.

Materials

- Copies of the book *The Magic Bed*
- Note cards
- Posterboard and markers
- Magazines

- "Do You Believe in Magic?" by the Lovin' Spoonful on audiotape or CD. Lyrics can be found in liner notes on album or online.
- Tape player or CD player

Vocabulary

Alarms • Beds • Literary elements • Literary genres

——————————— **Teaching Phase** ———————————

Warm-Up

Play the song "Do You Believe in Magic?" and provide students with a copy of the lyrics so they can follow along. After listening to the song, have students highlight, underline, or mark instances of magic referred to in the song. Ask questions to determine their ideas and thoughts on the magical elements of the song. Tell students that they are now going to read a story, *The Magic Bed,* and that it is another type of literary genre—realistic fiction. Go back to their vocabulary list and review words and definitions. Identify any new words and preteach these prior to asking them to read.

Transition

Put the Reproducible, "When You Listen to 'Do You Believe in Magic?'" on the overhead projector. Have students answer the questions listed. Then distribute copies of *The Magic Bed.*

Activity 1

Have students complete the worksheet "Activity 1: The Magic Bed" while reading the story (see Reproducibles). Follow the steps indicated on the worksheet. To determine prior knowledge and understanding, have students in pairs write on note cards what they remember from the story. This writing will give students an opportunity to review and check comprehension. It will also serve as a scaffold for reluctant speakers during the discussion.

Activity 2

Students will review what they have learned and extend their understanding of the text by sharing the pluses and minuses of the alarm bed. Students will write their responses on a **T-chart** (see Reproducibles). Working with a partner, students will discuss the bed's strengths and weaknesses. Students will be asked to change partners and complete the same activity.

Activity 3: Designing a New and Improved Alarm Bed

Students will use the information they gathered during the transition to create a plan or drawing for a new and improved alarm bed. You should explain the materials available to make the bed and what sort of devices might be successful in awakening a deep sleeper. Students will be asked to consider their own experience with waking up every morning for school.

Activity 4: Discussing the New Designs

Depending on the length of the class period, students will give their mini presentations either to the whole group or to a partner. Students will display and explain their designs, focusing on the components of their new alarm beds and why they chose those components. Listeners will ask questions after each mini-presentation.

Differentiating Instruction

Starting Up.   Students are asked to draw or cut out pictures from magazines. Match type of genre to short descriptions (in L1 or L2) with a partner. (Activity 1)

Beginning.   Students are asked to sort short segments of the story according to typical literary elements (in L1 or L2) with a partner. (Activity 1)

Developing.   Students are asked to draw and describe the bed using short phrases. Have them categorize types of works from a variety of genres (in L1 or L2) with a partner. (Activities 1 and 2)

Expanding.   Students are asked to draw the bed and include instructions on how to construct the bed. Identify the purposes and uses of particular genres with a partner. (Activities 2 and 3)

Bridging.   Students are asked to design the bed and write a story describing its usefulness. Analyze excerpts or favorite genres from modified grade-level material. (Activities 2, 3, and 4)

Assessment

Using the "Assessment of a Mini Presentation" chart, you will make notations about students' presentations by placing a check mark in the appropriate box (see Reproducibles). You should also write notes about students' presentations and the relevance of the listeners' questions.

Closure

You can discuss with the students how, when, and why many people use various kinds of alarms to awaken from sleep. Students would be reminded of what reading strategies they used when reading the text and encouraged to use those same strategies for reading other materials.

Conclusion

A directed reading–thinking activity is an excellent way to encourage ELL readers. It provides opportunities for students to feel successful and realize that reading is an interactive process. In this lesson, the teacher made the activity fun and the students were encouraged to be creative. The homework assignment further supports and provides additional practice with reading skills.

Homework

Students will begin this activity in class. They will be asked to write a journal entry reflecting on what they learned in the lesson. Specifically, the students will be asked to comment on their own new alarm bed designs as well as the creative designs of their classmates.

—————————— WHAT IF Factor ——————————

What if you have students who do not like to draw? Drawing might be a challenging task for some students. You can assure the students that the actual drawing is not the most important part of the activity. Students may use very simple drawings. To address this potential issue, you should show students samples of detailed drawings and simple drawings—both of which are acceptable. If students have adequate vocabulary, they could also make a list of features they would like to add to the bed along with an explanation in note form as to why each feature would be important.

—————————— Optional Activities for This Lesson ——————————

- Have students work with a partner.
- Assign each pair a set of characters from the story. Each student should assume the role of the character.

- Each pair will create a conversation on paper using the assigned character. Both students write a statement or question at the top of the paper. Then they trade papers with their partners and respond to what the partner wrote.
- Have students continue trading and responding for five to ten minutes. When finished, each pair will have created at least two conversations between characters from the story.

─────── **Teacher's Reflection** ───────

"Ninth-grade students enjoy activities that allow them to use their imaginations. Using the DRTA accommodates multiple intelligences and learning styles because all learners choose how they will approach the topic according to their own interest and background. Working independently or in pairs gives me time to scaffold instruction for beginning students. The DRTA can be used to introduce each of the literary genres required at this grade level."

─────── **Theory to Practice** ───────

The process of brainstorming and predicting can be used to activate prior knowledge since one student's idea causes other students to scan their neural networks for related ideas (Gregory & Chapman, 2002).

Lesson 5   Performance Indicator   Standard 2 • Grade Level 9–12

Domain	Topic	Level 1	Level 2	Level 3	Level 4	Level 5
Reading	Literary genres	Match type of genre to short descriptions (in L1 or L2) with a partner	Sort short segments of dramatic, poetic, or narrative works according to typical characteristics (in L1 or L2) with a partner	Categorize types of works from a variety of genres (in L1 or L2) with a partner	Identify the purposes and uses of particular genres with a partner	Analyze excerpts or favorite genres from modified grade-level material

Glossary of Terms

directed reading–thinking activity (DRTA) Structured and purposeful reading instruction that includes activities for responding to the text.

reading strategies Techniques that help students engage with the text and monitor comprehension.

scaffold Temporary support materials that aid language comprehension for beginning language learners.

T-chart A graphic organizer used to accentuate the positives and negatives.

Reproducible Activities

Now It's Your Turn!

Reflect and then respond to the following:

1. Identify elements of the lesson you might consider revising or modifying.
2. What are other reading strategies (prereading, during reading, postreading) that would work well with the lesson?
3. How can you include the variety of cultural literacies present in your class when you are selecting reading materials?
4. Pick two or three reading selections that are well known in the United States (poems, songs, nursery rhymes, etc.). Search for identical texts that have been published in other cultures or languages. Examine them closely to determine the literary perspective present. Compare and contrast with the U.S. versions.

Questions for Discussion

1. What are some ways to enhance literacy skills in both the L1 and L2?
2. How can you encourage building literacy in the home?
3. Describe some classroom resources you can provide that will entice students to want to read more?

References

Balderrama, M. V., & Díaz-Rico, L. (2006). *Teaching performance expectations for educating English learners.* Boston: Allyn & Bacon.

Burningham, J. (2003). *The magic bed.* New York: Knopf Books.

Gregory, G., & Chapman, C. (2002). *Differentiated instructional strategies: One size doesn't fit all.* Thousand Oaks, CA: Corwin Press.

Lovin' Spoonful, The. (2002). Do you believe in magic. On *Do you believe in magic* [CD]. New York: Buddha. (1965)

Palinscar, A. S., & Brown, A. L. (1984). Reciprocal teaching of comprehension-fostering and comprehension-monitoring activities. *Cognition and Instruction, 1*, 117–175.

Stauffer, R. G. (1970). *The language-experience approach to the teaching of reading.* New York: Harper & Row.

Visser, E., & Hanggi, G. (1999). *Guided reading in a balanced program.* Westminster, CA: Teacher Created Materials.

SECTION THREE

Planning for Brain-Compatible Differentiated Instruction

Unit Lessons

The two five-day plans illustrate sustained teaching. The lessons demonstrate how to plan and execute teaching over a period of time, aligning standards and teaching language through content. Use these plans as you begin to design instructional and assessment practices to reach *all* learners for an extended period of time. If you are a general educator with ELLs, these plans will assist you in differentiating your instruction over time in order to accommodate both ELLs and monolingual learners.

Remember the PowerPoints are available for you when you feel you would like additional information or resources on the topics covered in the book. Finally, the reproducibles can easily be copied and modified to fit your needs.

PowerPoint

Assessment for ELLS

Lesson 6 Creating Activities to Apply Content and Language Knowledge in Mathematics: Assessment

In order to monitor students' progress, it is essential to consider assessment as you put a lesson plan together. Assessing English language learners can be complex and challenging due to the various language proficiency levels of students. However, ELL assessment is necessary to aid administrators in screening, placing, and reclassifying students (O'Malley & Pierce, 1996). Assessing ELL students correctly will give students access to instructional programs that meet their needs. According to O'Malley & Pierce (1996) and Carrier (2006), assessment has moved from standardized tests and multiple-choice tests, which are very difficult for ELL students because of the level of proficiency needed to comprehend questions and to weed out incorrect answers, to alternative assessments known as *authentic assessment*. This kind of assessment consists of graphic organizers, oral reports, cloze tests, and performance-based assessments. These tools help to identify what students know, show student growth, and aid teachers with instructional planning (O'Malley & Pierce, 1996; Haley & Austin, 2004).

These alternate assessments are a much better method for ELL students because they depend more on the actions of students rather than on written or spoken language. This allows students to demonstrate their procedural knowledge and show their critical thinking level (Carrier, 2006).

In *Understanding by Design,* Wiggins and McTighe (2001) lay out a conceptual framework for instructional designers (view PowerPoint at www.sdttl.com/prof/docs/unitubd_files/ubd_ttl.ppt). The "backward design" model centers on the idea that the design process should begin with identifying the desired results and then working backward to develop instruction rather than the traditional approach, which is to define what topics need to be covered. Their framework identifies three main stages:

1. Identify desired outcomes and results.
2. Determine what constitutes acceptable evidence of competency in the outcomes and results (assessment).
3. Plan instructional strategies and learning experiences that bring students to these competency levels.

Before You Begin

Math, unlike other content areas, has a language of its own that sometimes transcends individual languages. The idea of numbers built on a base-10 system is the same regardless of the language spoken. However, there are many mathematical terms that are new to even native English speakers. The presentation of **academic language** vocabulary is essential in math, regardless of ESL level of English proficiency.

Another fact to consider is that the amount of English a student possesses does not directly equate to the amount of math knowledge he or she may have. In other words, a student who does not have much English vocabulary may have a great deal of number sense and may be able to calculate above grade level. The goal of every teacher should be to find out what students know, where they are struggling, and how to best take them from where they are to where they need to be, both in their English language development as well as in their math knowledge. In this unit, a variety of groupings, as well as teacher-facilitated small groups, help to accomplish this goal.

A helpful way to achieve accurate assessment that is specific to individual levels is through the use of a rubric. In Appendix M (p. 179), you will find a rubric designed to assist you in your endeavor to determine exactly how much each student understands and how successfully each student can use that knowledge to process measurement challenges and ultimately solve problems.

Scenario

Mr. Hall is an elementary general education teacher in a suburban public school whose fourth-grade class has twenty-six students: Seven are native speakers of Spanish, three speak Farsi, three speak Arabic, and three speak Vietnamese. The English language learners vary in their English language development from beginners to bridging. The beginners usually look to their peers who speak the same language for additional first language support.

Three of the five math periods are set up to have **learning centers** that students rotate through in one class period of sixty minutes. In the practice section of this plan students will utilize three specified centers. There are also whole-group lessons and activities. This is day one on this topic.

Standards and Intelligences

TESOL Standards

Standard 3 • English language learners **communicate** information, ideas, and concepts necessary for academic success in the area of **mathematics.**

Goal 2, Standard 1 • Students will use English interactively in the classroom.

Goal 2, Standard 2 • Students will use English to obtain, process, construct, and provide subject matter information in spoken and written form.

Goal 2, Standard 3 • Students will use appropriate learning strategies to construct and apply academic knowledge.

Virginia Standards of Learning: Mathematics 4.10 and 4.11

www.doe.Virginia.gov/go/Sols/math4.pdf

No Child Left Behind

Provide maximum opportunity for children to read and do math at grade level.

Intelligences and Learning Styles Accommodated

| Bodily/ Kinesthetic | Naturalist | Auditory | Logical/ Mathematical |

| Interpersonal/ Social | Intrapersonal/ Introspective | Visual/ Spatial | Verbal/ Linguistic |

Day 1   *Activating Prior Knowledge of Linear Measurement*

Planning Phase

Objectives

1. **Language:** Students will be able to share prior knowledge about linear measurement through various cooperative learning activities.
2. **Content:** Students will be able to analyze various examples and nonexamples of linear measurement.
3. **Content:** Students will be able to list facts and characteristics and create a definition for customary or metric linear measurement.

Materials

- Signs using metric and U.S. customary units
- Index cards

Vocabulary

Centimeter • Foot/feet • Inch • Length • Meter • Ruler • Width • Yard • Yardstick

Teaching Phase

Warm-Up

You will first explain orally and in writing the U.S. customary system. Students will be given some time to look over a list of vocabulary words relating to linear measurement (see Reproducibles). Students should choose one of the words and write it on an index card as well as draw a picture of the word. Then the students will be asked to choose whether their word pertains more to the U.S. customary system or the metric system and write their answers on their cards.

Transition

Students will then move to one of the corners of the room where you have placed signs saying *metric* or *customary*. In pairs, students will discuss their words and drawings.

Activity

Place students in groups of four. Have them look for examples and nonexamples of either the customary system or metric system using the **Frayer model** (see Reproducibles). They will examine and list or illustrate the examples, as well as the nonexamples, write down a list of facts or characteristics that the examples have in common, and create a definition for the customary or metric system of linear measurement.

Differentiating Instruction

Starting Up. Students will be given the option to work with another student who speaks their language. Because there are many choices throughout this activity, students can participate to the degree they feel comfortable

Beginning. The vocabulary words can be illustrated or described with words or numbers. These students can also be paired with other students.

Developing. These students are encouraged to participate fully in the discussion.

Expanding. These students will be responsible for writing out the characteristics and the definition for their word.

Bridging. These students will be encouraged to present their paper to the class. It may only be necessary to monitor students at this advanced level of proficiency

---

Assessment

You may want to use **anecdotal notes** to determine the facility and accuracy with which students are able to come up with examples and nonexamples for either measuring system. The Frayer models should be collected and displayed if correct information is written. Otherwise, students should have the chance to correct their inaccuracies either during the lesson or at a later time.

Closure

Groups report on something that they want to share about their Frayer model. Inform students that this is the first lesson in this unit about measurement.

Homework

Students should search for examples or nonexamples of the customary system and the metric system of measurement around their homes. They can either bring the items in or make a list of what they found.

WHAT IF Factor

What if there are students who are familiar with other systems of measurement? Allow time for them to share this information. Starting up students who may be in their **silent period** should be supported with visuals, manipulatives, and lots of **comprehensible input** to enhance language development.

Day 2   *Measuring Length Using a Metric Ruler and a Broken Ruler*

Planning Phase

Objectives

1. **Content:** Students will be able to use a metric ruler to measure the lengths of pictures of various items.
2. **Language:** Students will be able to discuss strategies for using a broken ruler and practice using one to measure different items.

Materials

- Ones cube
- Broken ruler
- Metric ruler

Vocabulary

Broken ruler   •   Estimate   •   Linear measurement   •   Metric ruler   •   Word problem

Teaching Phase

Warm-Up

As students walk into the class, give them a "ones cube" and ask them to look around the room for something that is the same length. Create a list of items for all students to refer to as personal references throughout the year.

Transition

Place the ones cube against a ruler and ask students to state its length in centimeters. Then show a broken ruler and ask if we could find the length with that ruler. Students share their thoughts.

Activity (Centers)

Problem Solving (tables with teacher)

Students will work through a word problem in small groups. The problem requires them to examine the possible ways to use a broken ruler (one that doesn't start at zero) to measure the length of the line. You will lead the discussion.

Personal Reference Hunt (around the room)

Students will be walking around the room in search of personal measurement references. For example, a student might find that a "ones cube" is exactly 1 centimeter long and wide. Students will complete as much of the personal reference sheet (see Reproducibles) as they can.

Metric Measurement

Students will use their metric rulers to measure the length of different items, draw different length lines, and choose the best estimate for different linear measurements.

Differentiating Instruction

Starting Up.   Word problem can be acted out. **Realia** (doll, broken ruler, etc.) will be used so that students can visualize the problem.

Beginning.   These students will benefit from the hands-on activities in centers.

Developing.   These students should be able to read the word problem on their own. They can be leaders with students who may need help understanding the problem or the task at hand.

Expanding.   These students can give everyday descriptive examples of how to solve problems using linear measurements.

Bridging.   These students can summarize and apply linear measurement information in graphs, tables, or charts to new situations.

Assessment

Using **observational assessment,** record on a sheet of paper with students' names listed how students are progressing. You may use check marks (✓) to indicate success and (✗) to show where more practice or support is needed. Leave space to make notes to which you can refer for planning.

Closure

Ask students, "What did you think about using a broken ruler? Was it fun, difficult, tricky? Tell a partner and then the group." Ask starting up students and beginning students to sort pairs of pre-selected items by length. (Use eight items, of which two are 3 inches, two are 4.5 inches, etc.)

Homework

Have students take home their broken ruler and select at least five items to measure. Have them draw or cut out pictures of the items they selected and label the measurements.

—————————————— **WHAT IF Factors** ——————————————

1. What if a student cannot easily measure the lengths of different items with a broken ruler? You can have these students measure other things around the room less precisely with the broken ruler, say to the closest quarter or eighth inch.
2. What if a student is really struggling with the concept of using a broken ruler? You can give that student a whole ruler and have them measure the items as precisely as possible.

Day 3   Equivalencies within the U.S. Customary System

—————————————— **Planning Phase** ——————————————

Objectives

1. **Content:** Students will be able to demonstrate use of a customary ruler or a metric ruler to measure the height and width of various large items.
2. **Content:** Students will be able to solve measurement word problems.
3. **Language:** Students will be able to use the Internet measurement games online.

Materials

- Customary ruler
- Metric ruler

Vocabulary

Brainstorm • Customary • Equivalent • Height • Length • Meter stick • Width

—————————————— **Teaching Phase** ——————————————

Warm-Up

Discuss and demonstrate with actual yardstick and meter stick the equivalent measures for one yard (36 inches, 3 feet) and one meter (100 cm, 1000 mm). List them for further reference. Present the story problem: "We want to purchase a TV for the math lab. If we measure the space that we have, it measures about four feet long. When we look at the magazine ads for TVs, all the dimensions are in inches. What can we do to make sure that the TV we want will fit in the space we have?" Allow students some time to work through the word problem either independently or with a partner. Students may choose to take a ruler or a yardstick to measure the TV and/or space. After a few minutes students share what they got for an answer. "Today we will be finding the same measures of length in feet and in inches."

Transition

"Turn to the person next to you and brainstorm all the different units of measurement for *length* that you know and when you might use them. Then we will share them out loud as a class. You have three minutes." Prompt the students by reminding them to consider both very small and very large distances. Write down on a piece of chart paper what students say.

Activity 1: Measure Height (around the room)

Students will measure the height or width of large objects in the room using U.S. customary units. Large objects can include the blackboard, bookshelves, tables, or any other item that is considered large. Students will measure the height and record it in inches and in feet on the "Measure Height" worksheet (see Reproducibles).

Activity 2: Computer Center

Students will play a measurement game on the computer located at www.funbrain.com called "Measure it!" Today they will work on measuring the metric lengths of different items. There are different skill levels so each student can choose an appropriate difficulty level.

Activity 3: Word Problems (tables)

Students will work with you in small groups to resolve word problems in which they need to find equivalent measures within the U.S. customary system (see the "Word Problems" activity in the Reproducibles). For example, Luisa needs ten feet of cloth to make a skirt. The fabric store only sells the cloth she needs in yards. How many yards will she purchase?

Differentiating Instruction

Starting Up.   Starting up students and beginning students can work on measuring height around the room. Allow use of L1 and students may partner with a student of the same language.

Beginning.   Key vocabulary in the word problems will be explained and demonstrated. These students may also work on the "Measure Height" activity.

Developing. Developing and expanding students may work on the computer center activity. Students at this level may need to have support reading the word problem and understanding the vocabulary.

Expanding. These students should be able to work on the computer center activity and given support when needed.

Bridging. These students can read the "Word Problems" activity on their own. The vocabulary will be explained as needed. They can also create their own word problems.

Assessment

Starting up students and beginning students will be asked to select one classroom item and use a metric ruler and a customary ruler to find its measurements. Developing and expanding students will exchange word problems and try to solve them. Bridging students will peer-edit their word problems.

Closure

Have students write a response to the following question on an **exit slip:** What two things did you learn today?

Homework

Have starting up students and beginning students measure the following: notebook, paper, book, pencil, and pen using both systems of measurement. Developing and expanding students can use visuals to create a word problem. Bridging students can be asked to create a game that uses measurements.

————————————————— **WHAT IF Factors** —————————————————

1. What if there are students who need more of a challenge? Students can challenge themselves to do similar measurements in the metric system and more precisely, again to the nearest quarter or eighth inch.
2. What if there are students who do not understand the problems or cannot even begin to imagine the scenario? It is important to have realia that relate to the word problem. For example, if you were using a problem about buying fabric to make a skirt, you could bring in a skirt as well as a yard of fabric.

Day 4 Citations

────────────── **Planning Phase** ──────────────

Objectives

1. **Content:** Students will be able to estimate and measure distances (for example, between the floor or door and a poster) accurately with the tool of choice (yardstick, ruler, etc.).
2. **Language:** Students will be able to define, calculate, and write down the difference between the actual distance and the required distance.

Materials

- Posters

Vocabulary

Actual distance • Calculate • Maximum • Minimum • Required distance

────────────── **Teaching Phase** ──────────────

Warm-Up

Ask students if they have ever heard of a *citation.* Explain that the fire marshal came to school to do a routine safety inspection and had to decide whether or not to give out citations to teachers because many posters were not within the required measurements. Share with students the actual requirements.

Transition

Ask students to look around the room and find an object that is three feet long. Give students some time to look around and then have students share what they found.

Activity

Once students have shared their findings, ask, "What tools did you use to figure out that those items were three feet long?" Encourage them to use the words *yardstick, meters,* and so on to be more specific rather than "I measured it with that." Then ask, "How can we be efficient about measuring?" Encourage them to use the larger tools for larger distances. "Today you will get a chance to be efficient by measuring the posters around the school. You will be like the fire marshal and protect our school by asking teachers to move their posters to a safer distance from the floor or the door." Show guidelines for displays and decorations in schools. Discuss *minimum* and *maximum*. Students will not be doing centers today but rather working in pairs to do the same activity.

Present a practice problem: "Mr. Lintner placed his posters eighteen inches from the floor. If the minimum requirement is three feet from the floor, how many inches does Mr. Lintner have to move his posters?"

Students form pairs that you have chosen and select a tool they will use to measure as well as which rule to concentrate on (for example, the three-foot-minimum from the floor rule). There are two different reproducibles, one with only two rules and one with four. More advanced math students will be given the more challenging worksheet. The class walks around halls with partners to measure posters and post citations where appropriate.

Differentiating Instruction

Starting Up. These students will participate by measuring the distances and focusing on only one rule.

Beginning. These students will also measure the distances, focusing on only a couple of rules.

Developing. These students will be able to work through the vocabulary of the rules by actually measuring and drawing out the posters and the rule which has been broken. They will concentrate on only one or two rules.

Expanding. These students will be able to focus on more than one rule. They will also help lead discussion during the problem solving at the beginning of the lesson. They may also create word problems for the bridging students.

Bridging. These students should be able to focus on more than one rule. They will share their solutions of the problems created by the expanding students.

Assessment

Check "Citation" worksheets for accuracy. Note observations during actual measurements. Do this repeatedly throughout the school year and see how comfortable students get with the measurements and finding the differences in distances.

Closure

Return to the classroom or math lab and discuss findings. Ask students, "What was easy about this? What was the most difficult part of this?" Have them write their answers and then discuss with a partner.

Homework

Ask students to walk around the school over the next day and see if they can estimate which posters have violated the guideline measurements. Have them make a list and bring it to class to share.

—————— WHAT IF Factor ——————

What if some students just don't get it? Some students will not be able to do all the parts of the citation because of the math involved, not necessarily because of the language. If this is the case, depending on the number of students, you can reteach this at one of the centers while the rest of the class is working on something else. You may also wish to have anchor activities available for this occasion.

Day 5   Perimeter

—————— Planning Phase ——————

Objectives

1. **Content:** Students will be able to identify appropriate tools to measure the sides of a school garden bed.
2. **Content:** Students will be able to draw a diagram of the garden bed with the labeled measurements.
3. **Language:** Students will be able to calculate and write the perimeter of the garden bed.

Materials

- Yardstick
- Tape measure
- Graph paper

Vocabulary

Clipboard • Data • Graph paper • Inside • Outside • Perimeter • Rectangle • Tape measure

—————————— Teaching Phase ——————————

Warm-Up

As students walk in, have them stand in a rectangular shape. Ask them, "What would the perimeter of this rectangle be if we measured it in people? What do you remember about perimeter? Does it measure the *inside* or the *outside* of a figure?"

Transition

Have students look at the word, "peRIMeter." Ask them, "Do you see the word 'RIM' inside the word?" Tell them that this is a good reminder that when we measure the perimeter of something it is the outside that we are measuring.

Activity

Try to take students outside to measure garden beds. Assign students in pairs. Have partners decide on a tool to take with them. They can take a ruler, yardstick, meter stick, or tape measure. They will also need a clipboard, a pencil, and a piece of graph paper.

Ask students what shape are the garden beds. As they walk outside, have students talk with their partners to decide how they can best organize their information so as to figure out the perimeter of a garden bed. Once outside in the garden, partners will choose a garden bed to measure in the unit of their choice. You will observe and help out as needed. Students will record their data and calculate the perimeter in whatever way they choose.

Differentiating Instruction

Starting Up. Students who are at this level will be supported by the direct use of materials and should be able to connect the vocabulary with real-life actions. Use of Total Physical Response (TPR) will aid in comprehension (see Methods of Instruction in Section One). State and confirm operation represented visually with a partner.

Beginning. Students who are at the beginning level will be supported by a direct focus on use of language in real-life contexts and should be able to connect the vocabulary with TPR actions. Relate how to solve problems with a partner following teacher **modeling**.

Developing. These students will be encouraged to use sequential language in describing the process of measuring the garden bed. Use sequential language to outline steps to solve everyday problems and share with a partner.

Expanding. These students will be instrumental in leading discussion in the whole group. They too will benefit from being able to set the abstract idea of perimeter into a real hands-on context. Give everyday descriptive examples of how to solve problems with a partner.

Bridging. These students will lead discussion in the whole group and be responsible for creating questions for the class. Explain how to use information for solving problems in everyday situations.

Assessment

You should observe the students carefully while they are measuring the garden beds. You can listen to conversations and make note of which students are converting inches to feet with ease or which ones are having difficulty keeping track of their data. Accuracy of how students calculated the perimeter should also be noted.

Closure

Have students look at the measurements they recorded. Ask if there are any differences in the lengths of the parallel sides. If there are differences, ask why they think that is the case (e.g., the bed was built with different-sized sides, we measured incorrectly). Tell them for the next class they will be looking at the areas of these garden beds.

Conclusion

The activities included in this unit lesson use content mathematics to teach measurement. The use of rubrics allows both peer and self-assessment and introduces students to connecting mathematics to everyday activities both in and outside of school. Creating interactive activities like the ones in this unit provides multiple opportunities to address an array of intelligences and learning styles.

Homework

Students will receive a worksheet of figures to measure and then calculate the perimeter of each figure.

WHAT IF Factor

What if students finish quickly? Students who finish quickly can measure a second garden bed or measure the same garden bed but in the other system. For example, if two students measured one bed in inches or feet, they can measure it again in centimeters or meters.

Additional Resources for Math Lessons on Measurement

- www.aaamath.com/grade4.html
  Provides resources for fourth-grade math concepts, including place values, decimals, fractions, measurement, statistics, and patterns.
- www.instructorweb.com/basicskills/measurement.asp
  Includes lesson plans, worksheets, and printable activities about measuring and converting distances.
- www.apples4theteacher.com/math.html
  Offers math games, interactive 100 number charts, money games, number sense games, and telling time games.
- www.teachervision.fen.com/measurement/printable/54604.html
  Provides worksheets and teacher resource books about measuring angles, telling time, and measuring weight and mass.
- www.internet4classrooms.com/skills_4th_original.htm
  Includes fourth-grade skill builders and interactive activities covering number relations equivalence, data analysis construction, computation operation sense, and fractions.

Teacher's Reflection

"Because this lesson is highly interactive by design, it requires a great deal of prior preparation. There is always the possibility that some students will not engage in the bodily/kinesthetic and logical/mathematical aspects of the lesson. It is therefore necessary to try to find alternative ways to engage and entice those learners. Another challenge is having ELLs with above-level math skills. I find that using anchor activities helps out a great deal with those students."

Theory to Practice

While engaged in solving problems, students must generate and test hypotheses related to the varying solutions they propose. These activities result in divergent thinking and exploring possibilities (Marzano, Pickering, & Pollack, 2001).

Unit Lesson 6   Performance Indicator   Standard 3 • Grade Level 4–5

Domain	Topic	Level 1	Level 2	Level 3	Level 4	Level 5
Speaking	Measurement	State and confirm operation, represented visually, with a partner in L1	Relate how to solve problems from models with a partner (e.g., "I need to put groups together")	Use sequential language to outline steps to solve everyday problems, and share with a partner	Give everyday descriptive examples of how to solve problems with a partner or in small groups	Explain how to use information from solving problems in everyday situations

Glossary of Terms

academic language Language focused on content.

anecdotal notes A method of recording activities that take place.

comprehensible input Students being able to understand the essence of what is being said or presented.

exit slip A series of short questions given to students at the end of a class.

Frayer model Example of a visual organizer that helps students understand key math words and concepts; a chart with four sections to hold a definition, characteristics, and examples and nonexamples of the word or concept.

learning centers Designated areas where learners engage in predesignated activities.

modeling Providing samples for learners.

observational assessment Assessment conducted through observation.

realia Three-dimensional objects that students can see, feel, and hold in order to understand a word or concept.

silent period An interval of time during which ELLs may be unable or unwilling to communicate orally in English.

Reproducible Activities

Now It's Your Turn!

Reflect and then respond to the following:

1. Why is it important to scaffold instruction and assessment for ELLs? What are some of the challenges that you may anticipate?
2. Create your own homework assignments for days one through five. How will you ensure that they are brain-compatible and differentiated?
3. Use the vocabulary list in the unit to create tier 1, tier 2, and tier 3 words. Follow the example used in Lesson 2.
4. Design a template for anecdotal notes.

Questions for Discussion

1. How would you redesign this lesson using the backward design model and the three main stages?
2. What are some other examples of alternative forms of assessment that would be appropriate for this unit lesson?
3. Why is it important to share rubrics with students *before* they are assigned a task or assessment?

References

Carrier, K. (2006). Improving comprehension and assessment of English language learners using MMIO. *Clearing House, 79*(3), 131–136.

Haley, M. H., & Austin, T. (2004). *Content-based second language teaching and learning.* Boston: Pearson Education.

Marzano, R. J., Pickering, D., & Pollack, J. (2001). *Classroom instruction that works.* Alexandria, VA: Association for Supervision and Curriculum Development.

O'Malley, J. M., & Pierce, L. V. (1996). *Authentic assessment for English language learners: Practical approaches for teachers.* New York: Longman.

Wiggins, G., & McTighe, J. (2001). *Understanding by design.* Boston: Prentice Hall.

Lesson 7   Supporting the Acquisition of English Writing Competence: Writers' Workshop

Story-Based
Approach to
Teaching Grammar

A writers' workshop provides students with opportunities to write about any topic while improving not only their writing but also their second language acquisition (Peregoy & Boyle, 2005). More importantly, teaching ELLs each phase of the writing process (pre-writing, drafting, revising, editing, and publishing) can help lower their affective filter since the process breaks down each step into more manageable parts (Peregoy & Boyle, 2005). In this approach to teaching writing, which implicitly uses a story-based approach to teaching grammar, the students choose their own writing topics and move through pre-writing, drafting, revising, editing, and publishing their work as if they were professional authors.

Writers' workshop is especially supportive to ELLs because students are encouraged to discuss their ideas, work with a partner or group in revising and editing, and interact verbally with others (Díaz-Rico & Weed, 2002). Moreover, the opportunity to write on self-chosen topics validates each student's experiences (Herrell & Jordan, 2008). Teachers can help ELLs become more confident about exploring their ideas by focusing more on what the student can do in writing as opposed to what they cannot. Marking up a student's paper in red ink will only impede that child's creativity. Peregoy and Boyle (2005) suggest focusing on ideas first and on corrections last. Additionally, the use of graphic organizers to aid ELLs throughout the writing process helps activate new language while simultaneously providing teachers with an opportunity to informally assess their students.

Writers' workshop is a framework for writing instruction. It includes a balance of writing to, with, and by students as well as strategy and skill instruction within a meaningful context. Explicit instruction takes place in large groups, small groups, and one on one with the teacher. Instruction takes place during the focus lesson, while students write, and during sharing. All students are taught to plan, draft, confer, revise, edit, and publish for an audience. Students write daily on topics of their own choice and curriculum-related subjects.

Before You Begin

It is important to first consider the various writing levels of all students. Your students will need to be introduced to pre- and during-writing strategies. These are strategies that will serve them throughout their educational lives. You may want to go online and view this PowerPoint before you begin planning for a Writers' Workshop: www.primaryela.info/uploads/Launching%20 writer's%20Workshop2.ppt

Scenario

Mrs. Floyd is a second-grade teacher in an ESL **pullout** program model. There are twenty-four students—nine boys and fifteen girls. All of the ELLs are native Spanish speakers, including two students born in the United States, having varying proficiency levels. Their writing and reading progress is reasonable according to the language acquisition timeline of two to five years for acquisition of social language and seven to ten years for academic language (Baker, 2002; Collier, 1995). This is the first day on this topic.

Standards and Intelligences

TESOL Standards

STANDARD 1 • English language learners **communicate** for social, intercultural, and instructional purposes within the school setting.

GOAL 1, STANDARD 1 • To use English to communicate in social settings: Students will use English to participate in social interactions.

GOAL 1, STANDARD 2 • Students will interact in, through, and with spoken and written English for personal expression and enjoyment.

GOAL 1, STANDARD 3 • Students will use learning strategies to extend their communicative competence.

GOAL 3, STANDARD 1 • To use English in socially and culturally appropriate ways: Students will use appropriate language variety, register, and genre according to audience, purpose, and setting.

Virginia Standards of Learning: English Language Arts 2.11

www.doe.Virginia.gov/VDOE/Superintendent/Sols/2002/English2.pdf

No Child Left Behind

Craft lessons to make sure each student meets or exceeds the standards.

Intelligences and Learning Styles Accommodated

Bodily/
Kinesthetic

Interpersonal/
Social

Visual/
Spatial

Verbal/
Linguistic

Auditory

Day 1 *Organizing Ideas: The Prewriting Stage*

Planning Phase

Objectives

1. **Language:** Students will be able to generate ideas before writing.
2. **Language:** Students will be able to write stories with the use of available technology.
3. **Language:** Students will be able to edit for capitalization, punctuation, grammar, and spelling.
4. **Content:** Students will be able to organize writing to include a beginning, middle, and end.

Materials

- KWL chart
- Yarn
- Divider signs

Vocabulary

Brainstorm • Feedback • Graphic organizer

——————————— **Teaching Phase** ———————————

Warm-Up

Students will be given a KWL chart (see Reproducibles). Students will fill out the *K* or what they *Know* about how a book is made. Have students share. Students will then fill out the *W* or what they *Want* to know about books or how they are made. Students will share their *Wants* with the class. Use of L1 and/or L2 is allowed.

Transition

You will read aloud *How a Book Is Made* by Aliki. Students can add to their *W* column. Then you read a story that you composed, introducing each stage of the writing process with the model on the overhead. The students will see an example of the prewriting (web), drafting, and revising stages. At this time students can ask questions. The word *prewriting* will be put up on the word wall and discussed before the next activity, with a focus on the prefix *pre-*.

Activity

Students will generate ideas for writing topics on sentence strips and post them at the front of the classroom. *Expanding* students will write words within their web or outline and may start to write a few sentences with them on the blackboard. You can leave up these topics so students can refer to them while they decide on their writing topics. There will be a long piece of yarn hung from the top of the blackboard all the way down to the floor with five divider signs: *Prewriting, Drafting, Revising, Proofreading/Editing,* and *Publishing.* Each student's name is attached to a clothespin and for now is not placed under any category. The students will focus on the prewriting stage today. Students will take twenty minutes to begin their prewriting activity, which can include an outline or a web.

Differentiating Instruction

Starting Up.   Students may use pictorial representations for their writing. The graphic organizer serves as a scaffold for students to help organize their ideas.

Beginning.   These students may also use pictorial representations or words. Students may be paired with a partner to assist in the use of the web.

Developing.   Students will write words to express ideas and can also work with a partner to assist in the use of the web.

Expanding.   Students will write words within their web or outline and may start to write a few sentences.

Bridging.   Students will complete their web or outline and may start to write their paragraphs. Students can refer back to the model draft to emulate what a paragraph should include.

Assessment

You should circulate around the room to informally assess student work. You can ask students questions to assess comprehension of the activity while offering suggestions to direct the writing process. Peers can also visit each other for feedback which will also provide you an opportunity to assess progress.

Closure

Students will share their ideas generated from the prewriting activity and will receive feedback on their writing. You can decide on feedback activities, which can either be a three-question survey used as an exit pass or oral feedback given to the students by their peers. All student names will be lowered to the *Prewriting* stage on the display in the front of the room.

Homework

Starting up students and beginning students can cut or draw pictures that depict their topic. Developing students should write two to three sentences on why they chose their topic. Expanding and bridging students can search for other stories that are similar to the topic they have chosen. If possible, they can list the stories and come prepared to share with the class.

WHAT IF Factor

What if students are at a complete loss for ideas or are hesitant to begin? Allow those students to discuss ideas with a peer. Sometimes students are better helpers and can encourage each other. Students can also read other sample papers for ideas or be given a picture from a magazine to help the student get started writing or jotting down any thoughts.

Day 2   *From Prewrite to First Draft*

———————————— Planning Phase ————————————

Objectives

1. **Language:** Students will be able to develop their webs into sentences.
2. **Content:** Students will be able to organize ideas using a graphic organizer.
3. **Content:** Students will be able to identify story elements with visual support.

Materials

- Timer

Vocabulary

Author   •   Collaboration   •   Editing   •   Elaborate   •   Illustrator   •   Revision

———————————— Teaching Phase ————————————

Warm-Up

Students will review writing concepts introduced in the Aliki book. Students will revisit graphic organizers, which are also titled "idea catchers." You should select a few ideas from yesterday's topic list and again model how to organize ideas into the web or other graphic organizers to remodel the prewriting process.

Transition

Create a word wall with the five phases of the writing process to help guide students. Students will suggest words to add underneath each phase to help them remember what happens during each part.

Activity

Students will try to develop their webs into sentences. You should stop and pause every ten minutes to show students the model paper and how to go from the web stage to the draft stage. The prewriting to draft stage should take the rest of the period. A timer can be set to check in and keep writers on task.

Differentiating Instruction

Starting Up. Students can either draw a picture or be given an illustration to serve as a scaffold to help begin writing.

Beginning. Students can draw pictures to help write sentences that relay their ideas. Students may be paired with a partner.

Developing. Students will complete their graphic organizers and can begin writing multiple sentences. These students may be able to help beginners.

Expanding. Students will begin writing their sentences and can also help students develop their ideas.

Bridging. Students should be able to have at least five sentences completed.

Assessment

Informal assessment is ongoing throughout the lesson, particularly regarding the comprehension of the following: (1) Are students using the graphic organizers to frame their ideas? (2) Are the more advanced students making other connections ("text to self" and "text to text")? (3) Do students understand how to transfer ideas from the graphic organizer to paper to form sentences? Positive **backwash** for you should result from this lesson.

Closure

Students can volunteer to read their writing. You can discreetly ask at least two students to volunteer their papers. Students who voluntarily read their stories will receive feedback for improvement. Some student names can be moved to *Draft* on the display in the front of the room.

Homework

Ask students to create their own version of a graphic organizer that shows their topic ideas. This can be as simple as a T-chart for starting up students and beginning students to something more complex and creative for the other proficiency levels. These are to be shared the following day.

WHAT IF Factor

What if you have students who may not have anyone at home to assist them with homework? This is sometimes the case and homework must be purposeful and tailored in such a way that students can complete the assignment when no one is available or capable of helping. This is why it is important to make sure homework is reviewed ahead of time in class. If possible, allow students three to five minutes to start homework in order to answer questions that may arise.

Day 3   *What Do Good Writers Do?*

——————— Planning Phase ———————

Objectives

1. **Language:** Students will listen for details from the list "What Do Good Writers Do?"
2. **Content:** Students will be able to select a graphic organizer and use it in the prewriting stage of their paragraph composition.

Materials

- Paper strips
- "What Do Good Writers Do" List

Vocabulary

Capital letters • Punctuation • Sentences • Strategy

——————— Teaching Phase ———————

Warm-Up

Students will be given a note card as an entrance pass with the question, "What do good writers do?" written at the top. Students will write down their ideas and put them in a paper bag. Students will then select one note card and read it aloud.

Transition

Students will be given a copy of "What Do Good Writers Do?" (see Reproducibles) while a copy is on an overhead projector. Students will go around the room and read one tip aloud. Students pair up and select one tip to write out on a sentence strip to present and hang up. Remind students to use their checklist, word wall, bilingual dictionaries, and sentence strips as references while they write.

Activity

You show students another example of how to turn a graphic organizer used during the prewriting stage into a paragraph and how to add details to their writing. Students should complete their first draft today and staple their graphic organizer to the front of their draft. One partner will be assigned to help their partner remember to read the "What Do Good Writers Do?" list after their draft is complete.

Differentiating Instruction

Starting Up.   Students can draw to depict what they think good readers do. You can also help sequence their pictorial representations in the order that the events occurred. Students may use their L1.

Beginning.   Students will organize their drawings and begin to provide more detail. Students may collaborate with another student.

Developing.   Students will complete their first draft and have a partner reread their work using the checklist.

Expanding.   Students will complete their first draft and reread their own work using the checklist.

Bridging.   Students can expand on their writing.

Assessment

Ask several students to summarize today's lesson and ask other students to tell the class one new thing they learned today. You can collect student work to assess the students' use and understanding of the checklist and of other available resources.

Closure

Put up yesterday's example on the overhead projector and ask the students to use their checklists to provide feedback for the anonymous writer. Students will move their names down to *Drafting* accordingly.

Homework

Students are asked to design a cover for their paragraph. You should show several book covers and model covers as samples. Encourage students to be creative; they may either draw, cut pictures, or retrieve pictures from the Internet. The cover should reflect the content of the paragraph.

WHAT IF Factor

What if students need additional support with writing at home? Because graphic organizers are now so readily available (online and various software programs), create a folder containing a wide variety of these. You can give them to students for extra practice. Some students may enjoy doing them just for fun!

Day 4   *Revisions and Proofreading/Editing*

--- **Planning Phase** ---

Objectives

1. **Language:** Students will be able to summarize the details in their story.
2. **Content:** Students will be able to create more details to make their story clearer.

Materials

- Problem–solution T-chart
- Writer's checklist

Vocabulary

Revision

--- **Teaching Phase** ---

Warm-Up

You should have an enlarged copy of the problem–solution T-chart in the front of the room. Students can discuss any questions they may have or problems they encountered during writing and give you ideas to write down on the T-chart.

Transition

The students will look at a student sample of writing on the overhead projector and will go through the writer's checklist. After students discuss the paper, you will ask them if they have anything to add regarding problems they have while they write and solutions they use that help them.

Activity

You should emphasize that today's lesson will be based on revisions. The students will discuss what they think *revision* means. Pose the following questions to your students: "Can you 'see' what is happening in the story? What details can be added to make the picture clearer?" Model the revision process with the students by showing them what to do. Students will then revise and edit their stories before publishing their final papers. Individually conference with students and review their writer's checklist.

Differentiating Instruction

Starting Up.   Pair students to discuss possible revisions.

Beginning.   Students will work with partners to discuss revisions. You may assist in this process.

Developing.   Students review their writing for any revisions they may want to make to their writing. Conference to review revisions and assist writers with editing. Students continue to collaborate with a partner.

Expanding.   Students will review their writing for any revisions and begin to work on their final drafts.

Bridging.   Students will finalize their revisions and can help you with conferences.

Assessment

Students will be given a 3-2-1 summary sheet in order to self-assess their writing process. Students will write down three things they did well in their story, two things they could work on a little more, and one thing that may be a problem. Students can write or draw pictures. You will ask students to volunteer their 3-2-1 sheets and discuss if time permits.

Closure

Students will share what they have learned from this unit. They will go back to their KWL charts and write what they *Learned* in the *L* column. This is an opportunity for students to share their observations of what strategies fellow writers used to improve their writing and how these changes made for a better story. Questions to pose to the group: "Did you use any of these strategies in your writing? How did they help you and your writing?" Student names should all be down to the *Revising* or *Editing* stage.

Homework

As a follow-up to the previous night's homework (designing a cover), have students create an end cover for their book. Again, these can be cut out, drawn, or retrieved from the Internet.

WHAT IF Factor

What if there are students who want to or are capable of creating a bilingual book (e.g., in Spanish and English)? This should be encouraged. If you are not familiar with the language you may want to seek assistance from the parents of your students. This is a very good way to build bridges between home and school.

Day 5   *Final Drafts/Publishing*

Planning Phase

Objectives

1. **Language:** Students will be able to write their final draft on the computer.
2. **Content:** Students will be able to select appropriate computer authoring tools (edit, save, delete).

Materials

- Students meet in computer lab
- Kidspiration software loaded on computers

Vocabulary

Clip art • Delete • Edit • Save

Teaching Phase

Warm-Up

Students will meet in the computer lab. You will model via the LCD projector a review of how to access Microsoft Word. Each student will tell you how to do something on the computer—for example, how to edit, how to save, and how to delete. The printers will be off and students will be reminded not to print until they have had a final conference with you.

Transition

Model the use of tools to save updates and have students begin writing their final drafts.

Activity

Students begin their final drafts. Writing is saved in their class folder under their student identification numbers. Conferencing with students is ongoing throughout class.

Differentiating Instruction

Starting Up.   Students may use the Kidspiration software to start with pictures and to write as many words as possible. You should assist with illustrations using the program options. Generate ideas before writing.

Beginning.   Students may use the Kidspiration software or can continue writing their own stories without the program. You can assist with illustrations as necessary and continue to assist students. Organize writing to include a beginning, middle, and end.

Developing.   Students will use Word to write their final drafts. Clip art can be added where appropriate. Edit for capitalization, punctuation, grammar, and spelling.

Expanding.   Students will write their stories and may enhance their work with pictures using clip art. Students may assist other students with Word, if necessary. Write a story with the use of available technology.

Bridging.   Students will also continue to use Word. Students may print and help others if finished early or expand their story by including a variety of authoring tools.

Assessment

All students are to turn in what they have completed for an informal assessment. Check each paper against the "What Do Good Writers Do" checklist. Have students self-assess their paper against the checklist and indicate whether they did each step or not. You can also turn the checklist into a rubric for a formal assessment with each tip used as a separate category.

Closure

Completed work is printed and used as models for students who are not finished yet. An extra day in the computer lab may be needed. All student clothespins should be lowered to the *Publishing* section.

Conclusion

The activities included in this lesson not only demonstrate sustained teaching but introduce young writers (second grade) to a sequenced procedure for creative writing. Students are guided and supported throughout. They are given time to reflect, review, and recycle their work from one day to the next. There are multiple opportunities to accommodate many intelligences and learning styles. Students can self-monitor their progress as they move through the five writing stages. The final "product" is available in their folder, complete with their own creation of a cover and end pages. ELLs are given the option of creating a bilingual book, thus showing further support of enhancing and supporting their L1.

Homework

Once students have had their individual conference with you, they can take home their final draft and put the front and end cover on their books. These can be bound with yarn, glue, or a spiral ring. These are to be returned the following day.

———————————————— WHAT IF Factor ————————————————

What if a student has been absent for an extended period and needs more time to work on this task? You can provide scaffolded support with visuals, manipulatives, and sample models for the student. This student will require one-on-one work with you throughout the lesson, and this can be accommodated with sequenced instructions and tasks, so that attention is not diverted from the other students in the class.

———————————————— Teacher's Reflection ————————————————

"This lesson offers multiple opportunities to tap into all the intelligences and learning styles. Writers' workshop is an effective tool in both mainstream and ESL teaching. Second-grade students get very excited about being described as 'authors' and it is especially gratifying when we invite parents to come in and listen to the students present their work. The greatest challenge for me as a teacher is making sure I can accommodate the range of native languages in my class when students opt to write their projects in dual languages."

———————————————— Theory to Practice ————————————————

Direct instruction supports all students, and is critical to students learning English as another language (Genesee, 2006).

Unit Lesson 7   Performance Indicator   Standard 1 • Grade Level 1–3

Domain	Topic	Level 1	Level 2	Level 3	Level 4	Level 5
Writing	Writers' workshop	Generate ideas before writing	Organize writing to include a beginning, middle, and end	Edit for capitalization, punctuation, grammar, and spelling	Write a story with the use of available technology	Expand their stories to include a variety of computer authoring tools

Glossary of Terms

backwash Feedback from students during the assessment phase, which includes questions or ideas that may not have been expressed earlier.

pullout ESL program model in which students are taken out of the mainstream general education class and instructed by an ESL teacher.

Reproducible Activities

The T-chart can be used when asking students to identify a problem and possible solutions. "What Do Good Writers Do?" can be made into a transparency or copied and displayed in the classroom.

Vocabulary List—Unit Lesson 7   185
Writers' Workshop T-Chart   186
What Do Good Writers Do?   187
KWL: What I Know about How a Book Is
    Made   188

Now It's Your Turn!

Reflect and then respond to the following:

1. Have you ever participated in a writers' workshop? If yes, describe your experience.
2. How would you use writers' workshop for older learners? Create a one-day lesson plan.
3. What do you think are some of the challenges teachers face in an ESL pullout program model?
4. What would you change in this plan? Why? How?

Questions for Discussion

1. How would you redesign this lesson using the backward design model and the three main stages?
2. What are some other examples of alternative forms of assessment that would be appropriate for this unit lesson?
3. Why is it important to share rubrics with students *before* they are assigned a task or assessment?

Additional Resources on Writers' Workshops

Calkins, L. et al. (2003). *Units of study for primary writing: A yearlong curriculum.* Portsmouth, NH: Heinemann.

Calkins, L., Hartman, A., & White, Z. (2005). *One to one: The art of conferring with young writers.* Portsmouth, NH: Heinemann.

Davis, D. (1993). *Telling your own stories for family and classroom storytelling, public speaking, and personal journaling.* Little Rock, AR: August House.

Fay, K., & Whaley, S. (2004). *Becoming one community: Reading and writing with English language learners.* Portland, ME: Stenhouse.

Fletcher, R., & Portalupi, J. (1998). *Craft lessons: Teaching writing K–8.* Portland, ME: Stenhouse.

Fountas, I. C., & Pinnell, G. S. (2001). *Guiding readers and writers: Teaching comprehension, genre, and content literacy, 3–6.* Portsmouth, NH: Heinemann.

Graves, D. (2004). What I've learned from teachers of writing. *Language Arts, 82*(2), 88–94.

Horn, M. (2005). Listening to Nysia: Storytelling as a way into writing in kindergarten. *Language Arts, 83*(1), 33–41.

Peregoy, S. F., & Boyle, O. F. (2005). *Reading, writing, and learning in ESL* (3rd ed.). Boston: Pearson Education.

Portalupi, J., & Fletcher, R. (2004). *Teaching the qualities of writing.* Portsmouth, NH: Heinemann.

References

Aliki. (1988). *How a book is made* (A Reading Rainbow book). New York: HarperCollins.

Aliki. (2008). *How a book is made* (A Reading Rainbow book). Retrieved February 6, 2009, from www.harperchildrens.com/howabook/bkstep1.htm

Baker, C. (2002). *Foundations of bilingual education and bilingualism* (3rd ed.). Clevedon, UK: Multilingual Matters.

Collier, V. (1995). *Acquiring a second language for school.* Washington, DC: National Clearinghouse for Bilingual Education.

Díaz-Rico, L., & Weed, K. (2002). *The crosscultural, language, and academic handbook.* Boston: Allyn & Bacon.

Genesee, F. (2006). *Literacy development in ELLs: What does the research say?* Presentation at the California Association of Bilingual Education's annual conference. San Jose, California.

Herrell, A., & Jordan, M. (2008). *50 strategies for teaching English language learners* (3rd ed.). Boston: Allyn & Bacon.

Appendixes

Sample Lesson Plan Template
(English as a Second Language)

Teacher _____ School _____

Grade(s) _____ Proficiency Level(s) _____ Program Model _____

Content _____

PLANNING PHASE

Content and/or Language Objectives
As a result of this lesson, students will be able to:

1. _____

2. _____

3. _____

Vocabulary

Materials

Lesson Outline

Content _____

National/State/Local Standards _____

TEACHING PHASE SEQUENCE

Warm-Up Activity

Transition

Activities

Grouping	Scaffolding	Processes
Entire class	Modeling	Reading
Small group	Individual	Listening
Partners	Guided	Writing
Individual		Individual

Activity 1

Activity 2

Activity 3

Differentiated Instruction
Starting Up

Beginning

Developing

Expanding

Bridging

Assessment

Closure
Review of this lesson

Preview for next lesson

Homework

REFLECTION PHASE

Learning Objectives
Were the content and/or language objectives met? How or why not?

Efforts to Accommodate:
Visual learners _____

Auditory learners _____

Tactile learners _____

Specials needs learners _____

What worked well? _____

What didn't work well? _____

What will you do differently as a result of this plan? _____

How might this lesson be improved? _____

One important thing I learned was _____

Brain-Compatible Planning Grid—One Day

Topic/Content: _____

Standards: _____

English Language Proficiency Level: _____

Date/Time: _____

TASKS	DESCRIPTION OF ASSESSMENT/ACTIVITY	✓	TIME FOR TASKS
Verbal/Linguistic			
Musical/Rhythmic			
Logical/Mathematical			
Visual/Spatial			
Bodily/Kinesthetic			
Naturalist			
Intrapersonal/Introspective			
Interpersonal/Social			
Auditory			

Topic/Content _____

Brain-Compatible Planning Grid—Five Days

INSTRUCTIONAL ACTIVITIES OR ASSESSMENT	AMOUNT OF TIME FOR TASKS	Verbal/Linguistic	Musical/Rhythmic	Logical/Mathematical	Visual/Spatial	Bodily/Kinesthetic	Naturalist	Intrapersonal/Introspective	Interpersonal/Social	Auditory	STANDARDS AND ENGLISH LAGUAGE PROFICIENCY LEVELS
Day 1											
Day 2											
Day 3											
Day 4											
Day 5											

Links for Multiple Intelligences Theory and Applications

http://gse.gmu.edu/research/mirs

www.howardgardner.com

www.pz.harvard.edu/index.cfm

www.pz.harvard.edu/PIs/HG_MI_after_20_years.pdf

www.gardnerschool.org

www.616.ips.k12.in.us

www.spectrumschool.org

www.prospect.org/cs/articles?article=multimedia_and_multiple_intelligences

www.jensenlearning.com/brain-compatible-learning.asp

www.atozteacherstuff.com/pages/1814.shtml

http://eduscapes.com/tap/topic70.htm

http://teachers.net/mentors/bcl

www.brainconnection.com/topics/?main=fa/brain-based

www.brains.org

www.crla.net/Brain_SIG_Newsletter_Apr07.pdf

http://ettc.lrhsd.org/archives/brain.htm

www.emtech.net/brainbasedlearning.html

Multiple Intelligences Activities Bank— Glossary of Terms and Strategies

academic language   Vocabulary needed or set as the goal for any given curricular unit or lesson. The language students must acquire to successfully reach academic outcomes.

guided reading   Teacher planned small-group instruction designed to help students develop reading strategies. Groups are flexible and can change to meet student needs.

KWL charts   Graphic organizers that activate prior knowledge and allow students the opportunity to get a clear picture of what they "know," "want to know," and finally what they "learn" from a given lesson or unit.

learning centers   Stations or designated activity areas in the classroom that are based on a theme or curricular content goal. Directions can be given to students and then they can work in the centers individually or in groups to complete learning tasks.

literature circles   Grouped reading discussion and analysis of a text in which each student is given or chooses a job or task to complete and share. Tasks change with each chapter or text, giving students the chance to explore alternate means of literature response.

living math problems   A kinesthetic activity that helps students visualize and establish a clearer understanding of a mathematics function or equation. Students act out or use manipulatives to show or act out the problems.

manipulatives   Tangible objects or realia that give clearer meaning to learners who need to have a concrete way to understand concepts.

Varied textures, shapes, sizes, and colors of the manipulatives can help raise student interest and concept comprehension.

read-alouds   Widely thought to be one of the most important strategies for literacy development, reading stories and texts to students can provide them with an understanding of story order, fluency, and a model for positive reading strategies.

scavenger hunts/knowledge quests   Activities created to provide students with clues and directions that will enable them to construct knowledge and understanding as they complete the given problems or activities. These activities can consist of movement, grouping, and even Internet searches for information.

storyboards   Graphic organizers that help students put a story in order and gain a visual understanding of the way a plot progresses.

story parts   The theme, plot, characters, setting, problem, and solution that make up a story. These concepts are essential building blocks for comprehension.

storytelling   Oral and kinesthetic presentation of a story or text that brings the ideas to life through dramatic presentation.

TPRS   Total Physical Response Storytelling is a strategy developed to use dramatic means to respond to text as well as give students the opportunity to demonstrate comprehension. This method of instruction is dynamic and can inspire enhanced interest in literature and reading.

Multiple Intelligences Activities Bank

The following is a chart of activities that will help you accentuate each of the intelligences.

Verbal/Linguistic
- Storytelling
- Creative writing/journal writing
- Oral debates or presentations
- Reading/guided reading
- Written responses to reading
- Interviews
- Creating questions about text
- Explaining or giving directions to someone
- Poetry read-alouds

Musical/Rhythmic
- Songs infused with academic language
- Culturally/thematically relevant music
- Rhythm use for memory skills
- Mnemonics
- Incorporating musical instruments
- Choral responses and readings
- Humming

Logical/Mathematical
- Patterning
- Problem solving
- Using graphic organizers
- Formulas/number sequences/calculations
- Deciphering codes
- Putting story parts in order
- Timelines for history and science
- Write your own recipe
- Puzzles and sorting tasks

Visual/Spatial
- Using and creating graphs
- Using art and images to draw conclusions
- Painting or drawing
- Pictorial responses to literature
- Video and live demonstrations of topics
- Mapping ideas and storyboards
- Creating, following, and understanding maps
- Incorporation of manipulatives for math
- Diagrams

Bodily/Kinesthetic
- Dance
- Role playing
- Sports
- Tactile activities
- Creation of learning crafts
- TPRS
- Living math problems (students act it out)
- Field trips
- Scavenger hunts/knowledge quests

Naturalist
- Drawing natural settings
- Interacting with objects from nature
- Teaching and creative writing outdoors
- Gardening with cultural and scientific themes
- Scientific experiments/chemical reactions
- Describing natural changes in the environment
- Recycling and environmental challenge tasks

Intrapersonal/Introspective
- Independent work
- Silent reflection
- Individual written/drawn reading response
- Journals or diaries
- KWL charts
- Connections to personal experience
- Setting, tracking, and evaluation of goals

Interpersonal/Social
- Group projects and experiments
- Giving/receiving feedback
- Peer-editing of writing
- Paired practice
- Learning centers
- Literature circles
- Interviews and conversation scenarios
- Mentoring younger peers

Tips for Working with English Language Learners

Today's classroom is a place where students of diverse backgrounds, experiences, and cultures converge for the purpose of learning. This learning environment is influenced by what students bring with them to school and by the quality of instruction that educators provide. In order for instruction to be effective, teachers need to know and understand their students. Teachers need to use this information for building a classroom community of respect, support, and expectations. This resource is designed for teachers who wish to adopt strategies and practices that will empower English language learners.

Develop a Positive Learning Environment

- Encourage ELLs to use their L1; provide opportunities for them to study their L1
- Recruit people who can tutor ELLs in their L1
- Provide books written in various languages
- Display pictures, objects of various cultures, and multilingual signs
- Encourage ELLs to write contributions in their L1 for the school newspaper
- Encourage parents of ELLs to help in the classroom, library, playground, and in clubs
- Invite ELLs to use their L1 during assemblies and other school functions
- Invite people from culturally diverse communities to act as resources and to speak to students in formal and informal settings
- Reward ELLs' attempts to communicate in English

Provide Students with Comprehensible Input

- Use visuals, realia, manipulatives, and other concrete materials
- Use gestures, facial expressions, and body language
- Contextualize ideas in relevant, real-life ways
- Tap into and access students' prior knowledge
- Modify instruction as needed using strategies such as scaffolding, expansion, demonstration, and modeling
- Encourage participation and interaction
- Focus on meaning making
- Maintain a low anxiety level and encourage risk taking
- Monitor ELLs' progress through interactive means such as checking for comprehension and clarification, utilizing questioning strategies, having students paraphrase, define, and model; verify that all students comprehend before moving on

- Modify your speech:
  - repeat, rephrase, and/or paraphrase key concepts and directions
  - speak clearly and enunciate
  - use shorter, less complex sentences for ELLs at earlier stages
  - use longer pauses
  - use intonation, volume, and pauses to aid in meaning
  - use idioms and slang minimally; explain when necessary

Help Students to Develop English Language Proficiency

- Encourage ELLs to join in group songs, chants, and poetry reading
- Encourage ELLs to participate in role-playing activities
- Expand student responses through modeling and expanded conversations
- Pair ELLs with a native speaker, when possible, if they need help
- Implement listening activities to assist ELLs in developing the sounds of English
- Encourage ELLs to communicate in English using familiar vocabulary and structures
- Provide opportunities for students to use English with varied audiences and for a variety of purposes
- Allow wait time after asking questions
- Practice sensitive error correction, focusing on errors of meaning rather than form; allow for flow of uninterrupted student thought

Back to School Tips

Know Your State and District Standards

- Review policies, regulations, procedures, and information specific to your teaching location
- Secure a copy of standards for teacher performance, administrative responsibilities of teachers (i.e., student attendance, grading, and grade books), and student achievement
- Get a copy of each curriculum (i.e., TESOL, state, district)
- Review procedures for field trips, school emergencies, and so on

Learn about Your School

- Grasp intricacies of your particular school; understanding the inner workings of your school will help you be more confident when you make decisions regarding management, planning, and instruction
- Find out who the important people are at your school (i.e., administrators, support staff)
- What are your school's vision, mission, beliefs, and goals?
- Does the entire grade-level staff do any planning together?
- Are there specific national, state, or local assessments and/or tests that you will give to certain grade levels? When? Can you get those booklets in advance?

Find Out about Your Students

- Where they live
- Are they from a low-income household (i.e., receive free or reduced lunch)?
- Which students are new to the school?
- What is the ratio of boys to girls in each of your classes?
- Are there siblings attending the same school?
- What are students' educational backgrounds (i.e., no school experience, held back, interrupted schooling, cultural characteristics of schooling in particular countries)
- Who are the guardian(s) (i.e., parents, aunt, older siblings)? What is their educational background? What is their literacy level?
- Which students receive special services (i.e., IEP, gifted, counseling) and who is their special education teacher?
- Review information about characteristics of students for the ages you are instructing; keep in mind that the children are unique and that information you read will only describe typical patterns
- What is each of your student's reasons for coming to the United States (i.e., war in home country, parent's job)?
- What other language(s) are spoken, read, and written at home?

- When necessary, learn some basics about each student's culture (i.e., inappropriate body language, traditions, role of parents in a child's learning, important religious holidays, role of a teacher in their culture)
- Talk with other teachers, if possible, who previously taught your students

Gather Materials and Locate Resources for Teaching

- Start at your school site to locate materials and supplies that are available to you through school funds (teacher handbook and/or student handbook, lesson plan book, grade book, electronic report cards, attendance materials, hall passes)
- Tissues, soap, first-aid kit
- Stock up on copy paper, transparency masters/overhead markers, chalk or dry-erase markers, board erasers, stapler and staples, paper clips, thumbtacks, rubber bands, scissors, masking/scotch tape, file folders, hanging files, writing paper and/or journals, primary-age paper, drawing paper, construction paper, chart paper, pencils, rulers, markers, crayons, colored pencils, hole puncher, erasers, and pencils with no erasers
- Purchase a large water bottle for you to carry and use throughout the day
- Buy or design rewards (stickers, certificates)
- Get multilingual/multicultural age-appropriate (label levels when possible) resources for students to read in their free time
- Ask school music teacher if you can browse through her things and borrow some of her music or song books in the future for certain units; find out about school performances
- Gather textbooks from grade-level teachers whose students you will be teaching
- Borrow or buy big books and sets of little books with corresponding tapes when possible
- Purchase or borrow music, cassettes, and videos

Prepare the Classroom Environment

- Arrange and organize furniture, instructional materials, equipment, and supplies for safety and convenience
- Create a warm, welcoming environment that will show students what an exciting and positive year it is going to be
- Post your name and room number near your door
- Post a map of the emergency route for students to follow in case of a fire
- Craft a "Welcome to ESOL" bulletin board
- Store rarely used equipment out of the way
- Consider carefully your furniture needs (appropriate-sized chairs and tables—height is right for the size of your students)
- Make use of every nook and cranny
- Set up an accessible library and include a cozy rug area if possible
- Make sure that the pencil sharpener and other high-demand supplies (i.e., Kleenex) are conveniently located
- Put AV equipment near an outlet

- Prepare storage systems for posters, manipulatives, realia, and bulletin board materials
- Depending on the age of your ELLs, you may want to structure your room so that there is "wiggle room" (places for younger children to move when transitioning from activity to activity)
- Set up the room for daily routines (age dependent). For example, blue tape in front of the door for students to stand on when they line up, places for names on chairs and on the table, a homework station near the door where students can easily drop off and pick up their homework
- Prepare and pin up bulletin board materials; calendar, alphabet, number lines, "Welcome" sign, student work display board, rewards bulletin board, student duties, the week's theme board, a word/picture wall, a visible place for warm-ups and objectives/agenda, and so on
- Decorate your room with multicultural and multilingual visuals; don't pick those that are stereotypical (e.g., Mexican with sombrero).
- Don't hang excessive decorations—an overstimulating environment makes it difficult for students to concentrate
- Set aside a small table or desk for daily teaching materials
- Set up teacher's desk in a convenient but out-of-the-way location
- Set up mailboxes or crates, learning centers for four skills (i.e., listening, speaking, reading, writing), class library, group working/reading area, and so on, avoiding high-congestion areas
- Prepare files:
  - labeled manila folders for ELLs national, state, and county assessments (i.e., IPT—international placement test)
  - labeled colored folders for each student's portfolio (i.e., one color for each class) which includes a section to record notes during parent/teacher conferences/correspondence, a checklist that shows how a student is progressing across the four skill areas, and work samples
  - substitute teacher lesson plans
  - holiday activities
  - helpful hints and ideas on teaching
  - school bulletins and newsletters
  - forms for discipline, incentives, and parent contact
  - personal reflection binder/diary

The CAN DO Descriptors for WIDA's Levels of English Language Proficiency

For teachers unfamiliar with the ELP standards, the CAN DO Descriptors provide a starting point for working with ELLs and a collaborative tool for planning. As teachers become comfortable with the Descriptors, the standards' matrices can be introduced. The CAN DO Descriptors are also general enough to be appropriate to share with students' family members to help them understand the continuum of English language development.

The CAN DO Descriptors expand the Performance Definitions for the ELP standards by giving suggested indicators (not a definitive set) in each language domain: listening, speaking, reading and writing. More targeted than the Performance Definitions, the Descriptors have greater instructional implications; that is, the information may be used to plan differentiated lessons or unit plans. The Descriptors may also apply to ACCESS for ELLs® scores and may assist teachers and administrators in interpreting the meaning of the score reports. In addition, the Descriptors may help explain the Speaking and Writing Rubrics associated with the ELP test. A distinguishing feature of these Descriptors, although not explicitly mentioned, is the presence of sensory, graphic or interactive support, through ELP level 4, to facilitate ELLs' access to content in order to succeed in school.

The CAN DO Descriptors offer teachers and administrators working with ELLs a range of expectations for student performance within a designated ELP level of the WIDA ELP Standards. The Descriptors are not instructional or assessment strategies, per se. They are exemplars of what ELLs may do to demonstrate comprehension in listening and reading as well as production in speaking and writing within a school setting. Unlike the strands of MPIs, the Descriptors do not scaffold from one ELP level to the next. Rather, each ELP level is to be viewed independently. Currently, the CAN DO Descriptors are written for the entire preK–12 spectrum. Given that they are generalized across grade spans, it is important to acknowledge the variability of students' cognitive development due to age, grade level spans, diagnosed learning disabilities (if applicable) and their diversity of educational experiences. Due to maturation, expectations of young ELLs differ substantially from those of older students. These differences must be taken into account when using the Descriptors.

Presented as an oral language and literacy matrix, similar to the format of the ELP standards, the Descriptors should facilitate educators' examination of the language domains for the five levels of English language proficiency. ELP level 6, Reaching, is reserved for those students whose oral and written English is comparable to their English-proficient peers.

CAN DO Descriptors

Grade Level Cluster 1–2

For the given level of English language proficiency and with visual, graphic, or interactive support through Level 4, English language learners can process or produce the **language** needed to:

	Level 1 Entering	Level 2 Beginning	Level 3 Developing	Level 4 Expanding	Level 5 Bridging	Level 6—Reaching
Listening	• Follow modeled, one-step oral directions (e.g., "Find a pencil.") • Identify pictures of everyday objects as stated orally (e.g., in books) • Point to real-life objects reflective of content-related vocabulary or oral statements • Mimic gestures or movement associated with statements (e.g., "This is my left hand.")	• Match oral reading of stories to illustrations • Carry out two- to three-step oral commands (e.g., "Take out your science book. Now turn to page 25.") • Sequence a series of oral statements using real objects or pictures • Locate objects described orally	• Follow modeled multistep oral directions • Sequence pictures of stories read aloud (e.g., beginning, middle and end) • Match people with jobs or objects with functions based on oral descriptions • Classify objects according to descriptive oral statements	• Compare/contrast objects according to physical attributes (e.g., size, shape, color) based on oral information • Find details in illustrated narrative or expository text read aloud • Identify illustrated activities from oral descriptions • Locate objects, figures or places based on visuals and detailed oral descriptions	• Use context clues to gain meaning from grade-level text read orally • Apply ideas from oral discussions to new situations • Interpret information from oral reading of narrative or expository text • Identify ideas/concepts expressed with grade-level content-specific language	
Speaking	• Repeat simple words, phrases and memorized chunks of language • Respond to visually supported (e.g., calendar) questions of academic content with one word or phrase • Identify and name everyday objects • Participate in whole-group chants and songs	• Use first language to fill in gaps in oral English (code switch) • Repeat facts or statements • Describe what people do from action pictures (e.g., jobs of community workers) • Compare real-life objects (e.g., "smaller," "biggest")	• Ask questions of a social nature • Express feelings (e.g., "I'm happy because . . .") • Retell simple stories from picture cues • Sort and explain grouping of objects (e.g., sink vs. float) • Make predictions or hypotheses • Distinguish features of content-based phenomena (e.g., caterpillar, butterfly)	• Ask questions for social and academic purposes • Participate in class discussions on familiar social and academic topics • Retell stories with details • Sequence stories with transitions	• Use academic vocabulary in class discussions • Express and support ideas with examples • Give oral presentations on content-based topics approaching grade level • Initiate conversation with peers and teachers	

130

				Level 6—Reaching
Reading				
• Identify symbols, icons, and environmental print • Connect print to visuals • Match real-life familiar objects to labels • Follow directions using diagrams or pictures	• Search for pictures associated with word patterns • Identify and interpret pretaught labeled diagrams • Match voice to print by pointing to icons, letters or illustrated words • Sort words into word families	• Make text-to-self connections with prompting • Select titles to match a series of pictures • Sort illustrated content words into categories • Match phrases and sentences to pictures	• Put words in order to form sentences • Identify basic elements of fictional stories (e.g., title, setting, characters) • Follow sentence-level directions • Distinguish between general and specific language (e.g., flower vs. rose) in context	• Begin using features of nonfiction text to aid comprehension • Use learning strategies (e.g., context clues) • Identify main ideas • Match figurative language to illustrations (e.g., "as big as a house")

				Level 6—Reaching
Writing				
• Copy written language • Use first language (L1) (when L1 is a medium of instruction) to help form words in English • Communicate through drawings • Label familiar objects or pictures	• Provide information using graphic organizers • Generate lists of words/phrases from banks or walls • Complete modeled sentence starters (e.g., "I like ____.") • Describe people, places or objects from illustrated examples and models	• Engage in prewriting strategies (e.g., use of graphic organizers) • Form simple sentences using word/phrase banks • Participate in interactive journal writing • Give content-based information using visuals or graphics	• Produce original sentences • Create messages for social purposes (e.g., get-well cards) • Compose journal entries about personal experiences • Use classroom resources (e.g., picture dictionaries) to compose sentences	• Create a related series of sentences in response to prompts • Produce content-related sentences • Compose stories • Explain processes or procedures using connected sentences

Grade Level Cluster 3–5

For the given level of English language proficiency and with visual, graphic, or interactive support through Level 4, English language learners can process or produce the **language** needed to:

	Level 1 Entering	Level 2 Beginning	Level 3 Developing	Level 4 Expanding	Level 5 Bridging	Level 6—Reaching
Listening	• Point to stated pictures, words or phrases • Follow one-step oral directions (e.g., physically or through drawings) • Identify objects, figures, people from oral statements or questions (e.g., "Which one is a rock?") • Match classroom oral language to daily routines	• Categorize content-based pictures or objects from oral descriptions • Arrange pictures or objects per oral information • Follow two-step oral directions • Draw in response to oral descriptions • Evaluate oral information (e.g., about lunch options)	• Follow multistep oral directions • Identify illustrated main ideas from paragraph-level oral discourse • Match literal meanings of oral descriptions or oral reading to illustrations • Sequence pictures from oral stories, processes or procedures	• Interpret oral information and apply to new situations • Identify illustrated main ideas and supporting details from oral discourse • Infer from and act on oral information • Role-play the work of authors, mathematicians, scientists, historians from oral readings, videos or multimedia	• Carry out oral instructions containing grade-level, content-based language • Construct models or use manipulatives to problem-solve based on oral discourse • Distinguish between literal and figurative language in oral discourse • Form opinions of people, places or ideas from oral scenarios	
Speaking	• Express basic needs or conditions • Name pretaught objects, people, diagrams or pictures • Recite words or phrases from pictures of everyday objects and oral modeling • Answer yes/no and choice questions	• Ask simple, everyday questions (e.g., "Who is absent?") • Restate content-based facts • Describe pictures, events, objects, or people using phrases or short sentences • Share basic social information with peers	• Answer simple content-based questions • Re/tell short stories or events • Make predictions or hypotheses from discourse • Offer solutions to social conflict • Present content-based information • Engage in problem-solving	• Answer opinion questions with supporting details • Discuss stories, issues and concepts • Give content-based oral reports • Offer creative solutions to issues/problems • Compare/contrast content-based functions and relationships	• Justify/defend opinions or explanations with evidence • Give content-based presentations using technical vocabulary • Sequence steps in grade level problem-solving • Explain in detail results of inquiry (e.g., scientific experiments)	

Reading

				Level 6—Reaching
• Match icons or diagrams with words/concepts • Identify cognates from first language, as applicable • Make sound/symbol/word relations • Match illustrated words/phrases in differing contexts (e.g., on the board, in a book)	• Identify facts and explicit messages from illustrated text • Find changes to root words in context • Identify elements of story grammar (e.g., characters, setting) • Follow visually supported written directions (e.g., "Draw a star in the sky.")	• Interpret information or data from charts and graphs • Identify main ideas and some details • Sequence events in stories or content-based processes • Use context clues and illustrations to determine meaning of words/phrases	• Classify features of various genres of text (e.g., "and they lived happily ever after"—fairytales) • Match graphic organizers to different texts (e.g., compare/contrast with Venn diagram) • Find details that support main ideas • Differentiate between fact and opinion in narrative and expository text	• Summarize information from multiple related sources • Answer analytical questions about grade-level text • Identify, explain and give examples of figures of speech • Draw conclusions from explicit and implicit text at or near grade level

Writing

				Level 6—Reaching
• Label objects, pictures or diagrams from word/phrase banks • Communicate ideas by drawing • Copy words, phrases and short sentences • Answer oral questions with single words	• Make lists from labels or with peers • Complete/produce sentences from word/phrase bank/wall • Fill in graphic organizers, charts, and tables • Make comparisons using real-life or visually supported materials	• Produce simple expository or narrative text • String related sentences together • Compare/contrast content-based information • Describe events, people, processes, procedures	• Take notes using graphic organizers • Summarize content-based information • Author multiple forms of writing (e.g., expository, narrative, persuasive) from models • Explain strategies or use of information in solving problems	• Produce extended responses of original text approaching grade level • Apply content-based information to new contexts • Connect or integrate personal experiences with literature/content • Create grade-level stories or reports

Grade Level Cluster 6–8

For the given level of English language proficiency and with visual, graphic, or interactive support through Level 4, English language learners can process or produce the **language** needed to:

	Level 1 Entering	Level 2 Beginning	Level 3 Developing	Level 4 Expanding	Level 5 Bridging	Level 6—Reaching
Listening	• Follow one-step oral commands/instructions • Match social language to visual/graphic displays • Identify objects, people or places from oral statements/questions using gestures (e.g., pointing) • Match instructional language with visual representation (e.g., "Use a sharpened pencil!")	• Follow multistep oral commands/instructions • Classify/sort content-related visuals per oral descriptions • Sequence visuals per oral directions • Identify information on charts or tables based on oral statements	• Categorize content-based examples from oral directions • Match main ideas of familiar text read aloud to visuals • Use learning strategies described orally • Identify everyday examples of content-based concepts described orally • Associate oral language with different time frames (e.g., past, present, future)	• Identify main ideas and details of oral discourse • Complete content-related tasks or assignments based on oral discourse • Apply learning strategies to new situations • Role play, dramatize or re-enact scenarios from oral reading	• Use oral information to accomplish grade-level tasks • Evaluate intent of speech and act accordingly • Make inferences from grade-level text read aloud • Discriminate among multiple genres read orally	Level 6—Reaching
Speaking	• Answer yes/no and choice questions • Begin to use general and high frequency vocabulary • Repeat words, short phrases, memorized chunks • Answer select WH- questions (e.g., "who," "what," "when," "where") within context of lessons or personal experiences	• Convey content through high frequency words/phrases. • State big/main ideas of classroom conversation • Describe situations from modeled sentences • Describe routines and everyday events • Express everyday needs and wants • Communicate in social situations • Make requests	• Begin to express time through multiple tenses • Retell/rephrase ideas from speech • Give brief oral content-based presentations • State opinions • Connect ideas in discourse using transitions (e.g., "but," "then") • Use different registers inside and outside of class • State big/main ideas with some supporting details • Ask for clarification (e.g., self-monitor)	• Paraphrase and summarize ideas presented orally • Defend a point of view • Explain outcomes • Explain and compare content-based concepts • Connect ideas with supporting details/evidence • Substantiate opinions with reasons and evidence	• Defend a point of view and give reasons • Use and explain metaphors and similes • Communicate with fluency in social and academic contexts • Negotiate meaning in group discussions • Discuss and give examples of abstract content-based ideas (e.g., democracy, justice)	Level 6—Reaching

Reading

				Level 6—Reaching
• Associate letters with sounds and objects • Match content-related objects/pictures to words • Identify common symbols, signs and words • Recognize concepts of print • Find single word responses to WH- questions (e.g., "who," "what," "when," "where") related to illustrated text • Use picture dictionaries/illustrated glossaries	• Sequence illustrated text of fictional and nonfictional events • Locate main ideas in a series of simple sentences • Find information from text structure (e.g., titles, graphs, glossary) • Follow text read aloud (e.g., tapes, teacher, paired readings) • Sort/group pretaught words/phrases • Use pretaught vocabulary (e.g., word banks) to complete simple sentences • Use L1 to support L2 (e.g., cognates) • Use bilingual dictionaries and glossaries	• Identify topic sentences, main ideas and details in paragraphs • Identify multiple meanings of words in context (e.g., "cell", "table") • Use context clues • Make predictions based on illustrated text • Identify frequently used affixes and root words to make/extract meaning (e.g., "un-," "re-," "-ed") • Differentiate between fact and opinion • Answer questions about explicit information in texts • Use English dictionaries and glossaries	• Order paragraphs • Identify summaries of passages • Identify figurative language (e.g., "dark as night") • Interpret adapted classics or modified text • Match cause to effect • Identify specific language of different genres and informational texts • Use an array of strategies (e.g., skim and scan for information)	• Differentiate and apply multiple meanings of words/phrases • Apply strategies to new situations • Infer meaning from modified grade-level text • Critique material and support argument • Sort grade-level text by genre

Writing

				Level 6—Reaching
• Draw content-related pictures • Produce high frequency words • Label pictures and graphs • Create vocabulary/concept cards • Generate lists from pretaught words/phrases and word banks (e.g., create menu from list of food groups)	• Complete pattern sentences • Extend "sentence starters" with original ideas • Connect simple sentences • Complete graphic organizers/forms with personal information • Respond, to yes/no, choice and some WH- questions	• Produce short paragraphs with main ideas and some details (e.g., column notes) • Create compound sentences (e.g., with conjunctions) • Explain steps in problem-solving • Compare/contrast information, events, characters • Give opinions, preferences and reactions along with reasons	• Create multiple paragraph essays • Justify ideas • Produce content-related reports • Use details/examples to support ideas • Use transition words to create cohesive passages • Compose intro/body/conclusion • Paraphrase or summarize text • Take notes (e.g., for research)	• Create expository text to explain graphs/charts • Produce research reports using multiple sources/citations • Begin using analogies • Critique literary essays or articles

Grade Level Cluster 9–12

For the given level of English language proficiency and with visual, graphic, or interactive support through Level 4, English language learners can process or produce the **language** needed to:

	Level 1 Entering	Level 2 Beginning	Level 3 Developing	Level 4 Expanding	Level 5 Bridging	Level 6—Reaching
Listening	• Point to or show basic parts, components, features, characteristics, properties of objects, organisms, or persons named orally • Match everyday oral information to pictures, diagrams or photographs • Group visuals by common traits named orally (e.g., "These are polygons.") • Identify resources, places, products, figures from oral statements and visuals	• Match or classify oral descriptions to real-life experiences or visually represented content-related examples • Sort oral language statements according to time frames • Sequence visuals according to oral directions	• Evaluate information in social and academic conversations • Distinguish main ideas from supporting points in oral, content-related discourse • Use learning strategies described orally • Categorize content-based examples described orally	• Distinguish between multiple meanings of oral words or phrases in social and academic contexts • Analyze content-related tasks or assignments based on oral discourse • Categorize examples of genres read aloud • Compare traits based on visuals and oral descriptions using specific and some technical language	• Interpret cause and effect scenarios from oral discourse • Make inferences from oral discourse containing satire, sarcasm or humor • Identify and react to subtle differences in speech and register (e.g., hyperbole, satire, comedy) • Evaluate intent of speech and act accordingly	
Speaking	• Answer yes/no or choice questions within context of lessons or personal experiences • Provide identifying information about self • Name everyday objects and pretaught vocabulary • Repeat words, short phrases, memorized chunks of language	• Describe persons, places, events, or objects • Ask WH- questions to clarify meaning • Give features of content-based material (e.g., time periods) • Characterize issues, situations, regions shown in illustrations	• Suggest ways to resolve issues or pose solutions • Compare/contrast features, traits, characteristics using general and some specific language • Sequence processes, cycles, procedures, or events • Conduct interviews or gather information through oral interaction • Estimate, make predictions or pose hypotheses from models	• Take a stance and use evidence to defend it • Explain content-related issues and concepts • Compare and contrast points of view • Analyze and share pros and cons of choices • Use and respond to gossip, slang and idiomatic expressions • Use speaking strategies (e.g., circumlocution)	• Give multimedia oral presentations on grade-level material • Engage in debates on content-related issues using technical language • Explain metacognitive strategies for solving problems (e.g., "Tell me how you know it.") • Negotiate meaning in pairs or group discussions	

Reading

Level 1
- Match visual representations to words/phrases
- Read everyday signs, symbols, schedules, and school-related words/phrases
- Respond to WH- questions related to illustrated text
- Use references (e.g., picture dictionaries, bilingual glossaries, technology)

Level 2
- Match data or information with its source or genre (e.g., description of element to its symbol on periodic table)
- Classify or organize information presented in visuals or graphs
- Follow multistep instructions supported by visuals or data
- Match sentence-level descriptions to visual representations
- Compare content-related features in visuals and graphics
- Locate main ideas in a series of related sentences

Level 3
- Apply multiple meanings of words/phrases to social and academic contexts
- Identify topic sentences or main ideas and details in paragraphs
- Answer questions about explicit information in texts
- Differentiate between fact and opinion in text
- Order paragraphs or sequence information within paragraphs

Level 4
- Compare/contrast authors' points of view, characters, information, or events
- Interpret visually- or graphically-supported information
- Infer meaning from text
- Match cause to effect
- Evaluate usefulness of data or information supported visually or graphically

Level 5
- Interpret grade-level literature
- Synthesize grade-level expository text
- Draw conclusions from different sources of informational text
- Infer significance of data or information in grade-level material
- Identify evidence of bias and credibility of source

Writing

Level 1
- Label content-related diagrams, pictures from word/phrase banks
- Provide personal information on forms read orally
- Produce short answer responses to oral questions with visual support
- Supply missing words in short sentences

Level 2
- Make content-related lists of words, phrases or expressions
- Take notes using graphic organizers or models
- Formulate yes/no, choice and WH- questions from models
- Correspond for social purposes (e.g., memos, e-mails, notes)

Level 3
- Complete reports from templates
- Compose short narrative and expository pieces
- Outline ideas and details using graphic organizers
- Compare and reflect on performance against criteria (e.g., rubrics)

Level 4
- Summarize content-related notes from lectures or text
- Revise work based on narrative or oral feedback
- Compose narrative and expository text for a variety of purposes
- Justify or defend ideas and opinions
- Produce content-related reports

Level 5
- Produce research reports from multiple sources
- Create original pieces that represent the use of a variety of genres and discourses
- Critique, peer-edit, and make recommendations on others' writing from rubrics
- Explain, with details, phenomena, processes, procedures

The CAN DO Descriptors work in conjunction with the WIDA Performance Definitions of the English language proficiency standards. The Performance Definitions use three criteria (1. linguistic complexity; 2. vocabulary usage; and 3. language control) to describe the increasing quality and quantity of students' language processing and use across the levels of language proficiency.

WIDA CAN DO Descriptors © 2008 Board of Regents of the University of Wisconsin System, on behalf of the WIDA Consortium, www.wida.us.

Multiple Intelligences Survey
Grades 4–8

Check (✓) each statement that applies to you.

Verbal/Linguistic Intelligence   TOTAL = _____

_____ I love books.
_____ I hear words in my head, before I read, speak, or write them down.
_____ I am good at word games, like Scrabble or Password.
_____ I enjoy playing tongue twisters, rhymes, or puns with my friends.
_____ English, social studies, and history are my best subjects.
_____ I like to show off what I write.

Logical/Mathematical Intelligence   TOTAL = _____

_____ I can add and subtract in my head.
_____ Math and/or science is my favorite subject.
_____ I enjoy brainteasers.
_____ I like patterns.
_____ I like to find out about new things in science.
_____ I like things that are logical.

Visual/Spatial Intelligence   TOTAL = _____

_____ I often see pictures when I close my eyes.
_____ I am sensitive to color.
_____ I enjoy doing jigsaw puzzles.
_____ I like to draw or doodle.
_____ I can easily imagine how something might look from overhead.
_____ I prefer to read when there are pictures.

Bodily/Kinesthetic Intelligence   TOTAL = _____

_____ I play at least one sport or physical activity on a regular basis.
_____ I like working with my hands to build or make things (like carpentry, model-building, sewing, weaving).
_____ I like to spend my free time outdoors.
_____ I enjoy amusement rides and other thrilling experiences.
_____ I am well coordinated.
_____ I need to practice a new skill, not just read about it or see a video about it.

Musical/Rhythmic Intelligence   TOTAL = _____

_____ I like to sing and/or have a pleasant singing voice.
_____ I play a musical instrument.
_____ My life would not be good without music.
_____ I can keep time to music.
_____ I know the tunes to many different songs and musical pieces.
_____ If I hear a song a couple times, I can usually sing it fairly well.

Interpersonal Intelligence   TOTAL = _____

_____ I am the sort of person that others come to talk to when they have a problem.
_____ I prefer group sports (like softball) rather than individual sports (like swimming).
_____ I like group games like Monopoly better than playing alone.
_____ I enjoy teaching others.
_____ I consider myself a leader, and others have called me a leader.
_____ I like to get involved in social activities at my school, church, or community.

Intrapersonal Intelligence   TOTAL = _____

_____ I like to spend time alone.
_____ I have opinions that are different from most people's.
_____ I have a special hobby or interest that I like to do alone.
_____ I have some important goals for my life.
_____ I consider myself to be independent minded or strong willed.
_____ I keep a personal diary/journal to write down my thoughts or feelings about life.

Naturalist   TOTAL = _____

_____ I have a garden and/or like to work outdoors.
_____ I really like to go backpacking and hiking.
_____ I enjoy having different animals around the house (in addition to a dog or cat).
_____ I have a hobby that involves nature.
_____ I like to visit zoos, nature centers, or places with displays about the natural world.
_____ It's easy for me to tell the differences between different plants and animals.

Areas of Strength (4 or more checks in any of the areas listed above):

What I learned about myself that I did not know before:

Multiple Intelligences Survey
Grades 9–Adult Learner

Check (✓) each statement that applies to you.

Verbal/Linguistic Intelligence   **TOTAL = _____**

_____ Books are very important to me.
_____ I hear words in my head, before I read, speak, or write them down.
_____ I am good at word games, like Scrabble or Password.
_____ I enjoy entertaining others or myself with tongue twisters, rhymes, or puns.
_____ English, social studies, and history are easier for me than math and science.
_____ I have recently written something that I am especially proud of.

Logical/Mathematical Intelligence   **TOTAL = _____**

_____ I can easily compute numbers in my head.
_____ Math and/or science are among my favorite subjects in school.
_____ I enjoy brainteasers or games that require logical thinking.
_____ My mind searches for patterns and regularities in things.
_____ I am interested in new developments in science.
_____ I believe that almost everything has a logical explanation.

Visual/Spatial Intelligence   **TOTAL = _____**

_____ I often see clear visual images when I close my eyes.
_____ I am sensitive to color.
_____ I enjoy doing jigsaw puzzles.
_____ I like to draw or doodle.
_____ I can easily imagine how something might look from a bird's-eye view.
_____ I prefer looking at reading material with lots of illustrations.

Bodily/Kinesthetic Intelligence   **TOTAL = _____**

_____ I participate in at least one sport or physical activity on a regular basis.
_____ I like working with my hands on concrete activities (like carpentry, model-building, sewing, weaving).
_____ I like to spend my free time outdoors.
_____ I enjoy amusement rides and other thrilling experiences.
_____ I would describe myself as well coordinated.
_____ I need to practice a new skill, not just read about it or see a video about it.

Musical/Rhythmic Intelligence   TOTAL = _____

_____ I have a pleasant singing voice.
_____ I play a musical instrument.
_____ My life would not be so great without music.
_____ I can easily keep time to music with a simple percussion instrument,
_____ I know the tunes to many different songs and musical pieces.
_____ If I hear a musical selection a couple times, I can usually sing it fairly accurately.

Interpersonal Intelligence   TOTAL = _____

_____ I am the sort of person that others come to for advice.
_____ I prefer group sports (like softball) rather than individual sports (like swimming).
_____ I like group games like Monopoly better than individual entertainment.
_____ I enjoy the challenge of teaching others how to do something.
_____ I consider myself a leader, and others have called me a leader.
_____ I like to get involved in social activities at my school, church, or community.

Intrapersonal Intelligence   TOTAL = _____

_____ I regularly spend time alone, reflecting or thinking about important questions.
_____ I have opinions that set me apart from the crowd.
_____ I have a special hobby or interest that I like to do alone.
_____ I have some important goals for my life that I regularly think about.
_____ I consider myself to be independent minded or strong willed.
_____ I keep a personal diary or journal to write down my thoughts or feelings about life.

Naturalist   TOTAL = _____

_____ I have a garden and/or like to work outdoors.
_____ I really like to go backpacking and hiking.
_____ I enjoy having different animals around the house (in addition to a dog or cat).
_____ I have a hobby that involves nature.
_____ I like to visit zoos, nature centers, or places with displays about the natural world.
_____ It's easy for me to tell the difference between different kinds of plants and animals.

Areas of Strength (4 or more checks):

What I learned about myself that I did not know before:

Study Guide Questions

It has become quite a trend recently for school districts to adopt a book and use it for professional development purposes throughout the academic school year. *Brain-Compatible Differentiated Instruction for English Language Learners* can easily be used for such a purpose. You may wish to create a series of workshops that meet four times a year. Each teacher would be given the book at the first session as well as a binder to be used for reflective journaling and as a repository of additional resources gathered throughout the discussions. Consider creating chat rooms, blogs, or other electronic discussion boards with guiding questions taken from the lists that follow. Teachers should act as leaders and determine how best to organize these meetings. When the meetings and discussions are teacher-led, the discussion will probably be richer and more meaningful, while also allowing teachers to act as school leaders.

Rather than just having teachers meet and answer the questions, advance work to prepare might include the following:

- Role plays of major ideas presented
- Methods to prompt teacher journal entries of their real-life experiences that can be related to ideas in the book
- Frameworks for teachers to work in teams to prepare and discuss questions
- Arrangements for different teachers or teams of teachers to lead the discussion so everyone shares their expertise and experiences

Brain-Compatible Teaching and Learning

- What is brain-compatible teaching and learning?
- How can teachers work to ensure that their instruction and assessment are brain-compatible?
- How does brain-compatible teaching and learning benefit English language learners? Explain and provide examples.
- In what ways can brain-compatible teaching ensure that teachers are reaching all learners?
- What impact does planning have on brain-compatible teaching and learning?

Brain-Compatible Theories of Teaching and Learning: Multiple Intelligences and Learning Styles

- Why is it so important for teachers to understand how our own intelligences and preferred learning styles have an influence on the way we teach? Cite an example of your own experience.
- What are some ways to identify students' intelligences (strengths and weaknesses) when language and culture are a barrier?
- Make a list of strategies that will be useful for building on the strengths of multiple intelligences while working with English language learners.

- Create a graphic organizer depicting at least five intelligences and two learning styles. Include matching characteristics and activities.
- Discuss ways to incorporate the teaching strategies highlighted in the accompanying PowerPoint on brain-compatible teaching.

Differentiating Instruction

- What are the key elements of managing and planning in a differentiated classroom? Use the lesson plan template and create a one-day plan with differentiated activities.
- Describe the relationship between anchor activities and managing a differentiated classroom.
- Give examples of the three aspects of differentiating: content, process, and products.
- What are some ways to get know to know the backgrounds of your students? How can this information help plan instruction and assessment?
- Partner with a colleague and create at least four anchor activities. Describe when and how they would be useful.

Meeting the Needs of English Language Learners

- Why is it important to understand the five stages of developing English language proficiency?
- Make a list of ways you can check for comprehension with students still experiencing a silent period.
- Create a plan for building bridges to parental involvement. Decide when and how these activities can be done.
- In what ways can you provide a print-rich classroom environment for all students, especially English language learners?
- What are some helpful tips about working with English language learners to share with mainstream education teachers?

ESL Standards for Pre-K–12 Students and English Language Proficiency Standards

- In what ways do the ESL Standards consider the cultural backgrounds of English language learners? Cite specific examples.
- Describe how to align local and state standards with the national standards. Why is this important?
- Create a standards-based activity and an assessment that incorporate all four skills (listening, speaking, reading, and writing). Discuss the steps you took. How were your decisions made?
- Why is it important for mainstream educators to be familiar with the ESL Standards?

TESOL Performance Indicators and How to Read Them

- What are Performance Indicators and why are they necessary in planning for instruction and assessment?
- How do Performance Indicators influence student progress in language and content learning?
- Select one of the Performance Indicators used in the lessons. Identify content, language, function, and support or strategy.
- Discuss the importance of how the Performance Indicators are organized.
- Explain how to read the Performance Indicators.

World-Class Instructional Design and Assessment (WIDA)

- What is the WIDA consortium? Is your state a member? Go online and search for more information about WIDA.
- What are the CAN DO Descriptors? How can they further support the academic challenges facing English language learners?
- In what ways do the Descriptors help with differentiating instruction?
- How are the Descriptors sensory-preferred and interactive? Give specific examples.
- As a group, decide how to use the Descriptors. When? With whom? Why? In what content areas?

Second Language Acquisition Theory

- Discuss your interpretation of BICS and CALP.
- What are some ways to promote both BICS and CALP simultaneously?
- Discuss the most important characteristics of the Cummins' Quadrant Model.
- Review the PowerPoint on Second Language Acquisition. Select three topics of interest. Create a list of questions you still might have.
- Go online and read more about Dr. James Cummins. Discuss his research on English language learners and the impact it has had on education in the United States.

Program Models of Instruction

- How are the SIOP and Sheltered Content-Based Instruction effective models for teaching English language learners?
- Write a brief description and then discuss each of the models described in this section.
- What are the similarities between the SIOP and content-based models?
- Which program do you prefer? Why?
- Identify a program model that is being used in your school district. Interview at least three teachers and ask their views (positive and negative). Discuss with your group.

Methods of Instruction

- Create a graphic organizer that demonstrates the methods covered in this section.
- Explain why Total Physical Response (TPR) is an effective approach for working with English language learners.
- Describe the usefulness of Cognitive Academic Language Learning Approach (CALLA).
- Go online and search for information on Total Physical Response Storytelling (TPRS). How would you incorporate this as an instructional strategy?
- What do you believe are effective methods of instruction? Why?

Classroom Management

- How do you distinguish between classroom management and classroom discipline?
- What are some guidelines to follow when forming groups in a classroom with different language proficiency levels?
- Describe ways to establish nonverbal cues?
- Create a list of classroom management rules for each of the following: elementary, middle, and high school.
- Design a centers activity that utilizes at least four areas of the room (i.e., computer, reading, hands-on manipulatives).

Classroom Discipline

- Discuss the importance of *how* classroom discipline rules are worded. Create a list of five rules and discuss with your colleagues.
- What are some ways to teach students skills, motivation, and positive attitudes toward school and their work?
- Create a scenario that involves a discipline problem that occurred in a classroom. Write it down and share with the group. Ask for alternative solutions on how to handle the situation.
- In what way does planning affect classroom discipline?
- Identify a school in your community. Determine what the schoolwide policy is about discipline (i.e., fighting, bullying, etc.).

Appendix M

Reproducible Activities

Vocabulary List—Lesson 1

1. Sun
2. Jupiter
3. Mercury
4. Earth
5. Neptune
6. Saturn
7. Mars
8. Uranus
9. Venus
10. Moon

11. Gravity
12. Description
13. Rotate
14. Revolve
15. Closer to
16. Farther away
17. Distance
18. Makeup
19. Size
20. Solar system

The Solar System

Directions: Using the resources available, complete the graphic organizer with your partner.

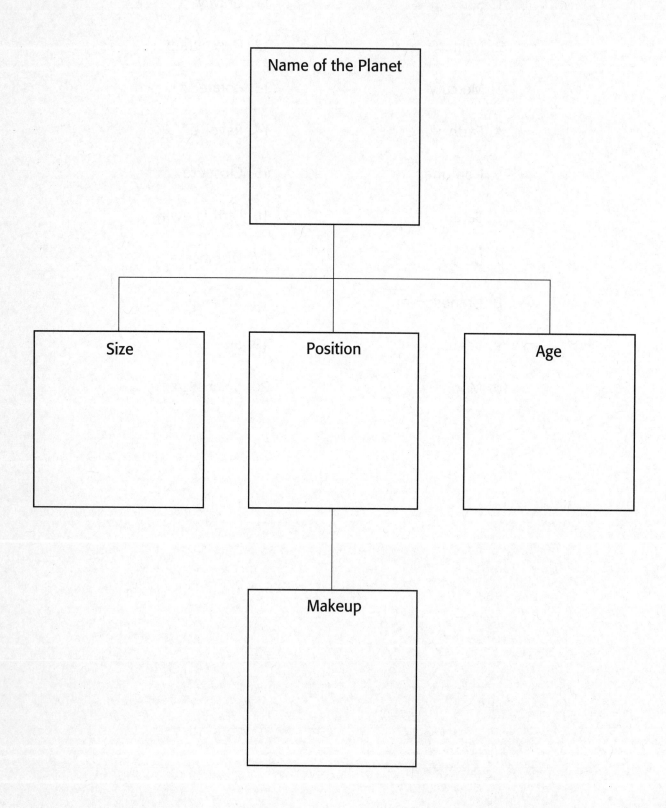

Name of the Planet

Size

Position

Age

Makeup

Solar System Activity

Directions: Put the planets in order in relation to their distance from the sun.
Cut out the planets and put them in order.

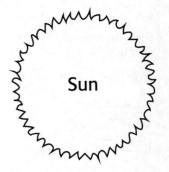

Sun

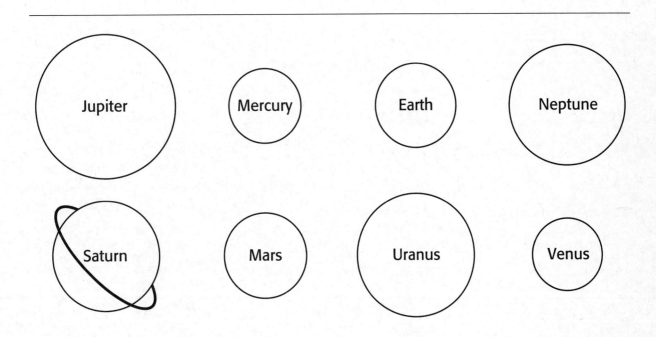

Jupiter

Mercury

Earth

Neptune

Saturn

Mars

Uranus

Venus

Solar System Checklist

Closure Activity

	Highly Evident (4)	(3)	Somewhat Evident (2)	(1)	Not Evident (0)
Draws planets					
Labels planets					
Writes characteristics of planets					
Writes about the sun and moon					
Places planets in order					

Lesson 1 Homework
The Solar System

Name: _____ **Date:** _____

1. Name the planets in the solar system in order.

2. Write a three-sentence description about two of the planets, the sun, or the moon.

Vocabulary List—Lesson 2

Tier 1

1. Police officer

2. Farmer

3. Banker

4. Accountant

5. Athlete

6. Rock star

7. Bus driver

8. Waiter/Waitress

9. Pilot

10. Artist

11. Book publisher

12. Car salesperson

13. Car mechanic

14. Construction worker

15. Jobs

16. Careers

Tier 2

1. Depends on

2. Provides a service

3. Goods

4. Services

5. Economics

Tier 3

1. Tariff

2. Revenue

3. Interdependence

Interdependence Chains

Directions: Fill in each link with jobs that are interdependent and give a reason why they need each other.

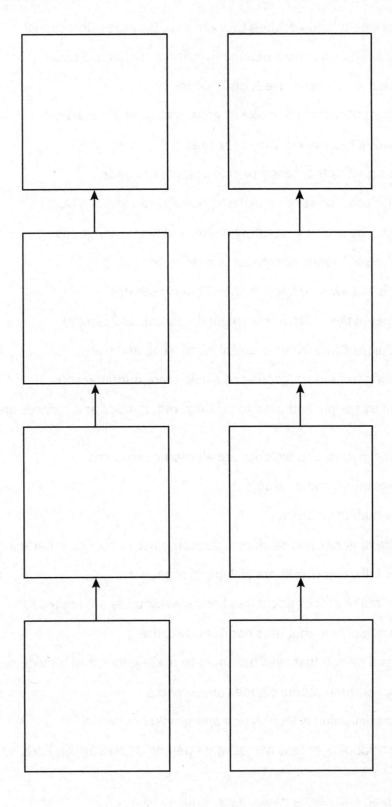

Economics Review Sheet

Name: _____

1. Doctors take care of people when they are sick. They provide a service.

2. Basic needs are things people need to live (food, shelter, clothing).

3. Money is used to buy basic needs and wants.

4. Goods are things that people make or grow that can be purchased.

5. Games are not a basic need. They are wants.

6. Services are activities that satisfy people's wants or needs.

7. A person who uses money to purchase goods or services is a buyer.

8. Things people make or use to satisfy needs and wants are goods.

9. A person who sells goods or services is a seller.

10. Money that is put away to keep or spend later is savings.

11. There are three types of resources (natural, human, and capital).

12. Natural resources come from nature, like soil, coal, and water.

13. People working to produce goods and services are human resources.

14. Goods made by people and used to produce other goods and services are called capital resources.

15. Hammers, computers, and factories are all capital resources.

16. Lawn mowers are a capital resource.

17. Miners are a human resource.

18. The exchange of goods and services without the use of money is bartering.

19. Coins, paper bills, and checks are all type of money.

20. People must make economic choices because resources are limited.

21. A consumer is a person that uses goods and services.

22. A producer is a person that uses resources to make goods and provide services.

23. Resources are used to produce goods and services.

24. Economic specialization is focusing on one product or service.

25. Economic interdependence is two or more people depending on each other for goods and services.

Source: Adapted from Chesterfield County Public Schools, VA, 2006.

Careers and Interdependence Worksheet

Directions: OPTION A—While viewing the video *A Career for Buster,* put a check ✓ next to each career you identify.

OPTION B—Write a description of three careers and include goods and services that are related to them.

_____   _____

_____   _____

_____   _____

_____   _____

_____   _____

_____   _____

Vocabulary List—Lesson 3

1. Plant cells
2. Animal cells
3. Ribosome
4. Mitochondria
5. Nucleolus
6. Lysosome
7. Cell membrane
8. Cell wall
9. Vacuole
10. Cytoplasm
11. Endoplasmic reticulum
12. Nucleus
13. Chloroplast
14. Store
15. Waste
16. Digest
17. Process

Activity 1 Questions
What Do You Know about Cells?

Teacher cuts up questions and hands them out as students enter.
Students post answers on tagboard.

Are cells alive? Why do you think this? Take a guess! ☺ Write your ideas down here and then post them on the poster on the wall.

Are cells located in your body? If you think so, where are they located? Take a guess. ☺ Write your ideas down here and then post them on the poster on the wall.

Do plants and animals have cells? Take a guess! ☺ Write your ideas down here and then post them on the poster on the wall.

Do corks have cells? (An actual piece of cork is attached here.) Take a guess! ☺ Write your ideas down here and then post them on the poster on the wall.

Word Chart

Name: _____ **Date:** _____

Directions

1. Your teacher will assign everyone a different vocabulary word.

2. During class, you will write down *other* words you hear or read that help you describe your vocabulary word.

   (You may also include two words to describe your vocabulary word from your first language.) ☺

3. In the other box, you will draw a picture of what the word reminds you of or looks like in your mind.

Vocabulary Word
_____

Words to Describe Your Word	Draw a Picture

Mini Lab: Cell Observation

Name: _____ **Date:** _____

Directions: View the plant and animal cell slides at one of the three powers. Draw and color what you see at each power level.

Step-by-Step Directions for Using the Microscope

1. Place the animal or plant slide in the slide holder.
2. **Center** or put the slide in the **middle.**
3. Which lens are you using? **Low, medium, or high?** Write it down in the right box. (**Look at the numbers.**)
4. Do not touch the slide to the lens.
5. Focus your lens.
6. Draw what you see.
7. Using these techniques, remove the slide and view the other animal cell slide, and then put the microscope away.

40× Animal Cell	**100×** Animal Cell	**400×** Animal Cell
40× Plant Cell	**100×** Plant Cell	**400×** Plant Cell

Name: _____ **Date:** _____

Venn Diagram
Comparing and Contrasting

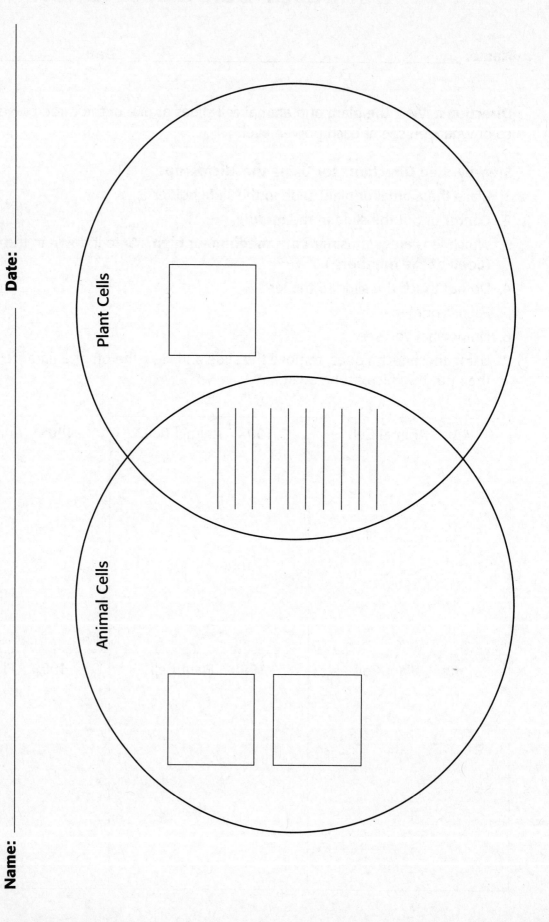

Plant Cells

Animal Cells

Drawing a Plant Cell

Name: _____ **Date:** _____

Directions: Draw a plant cell in the box. Label as many parts as you can. You can use your book and our class worksheets. Identify each part by coloring it the color indicated in the word box.

cell membrane (yellow)	cell wall (blue)	chloroplast (green)	cytoplasm (light green)
mitochondria (orange)	nucleus (red)	ribosome (black)	vacuole (brown)

Plant Cell

Drawing an Animal Cell

Name: _____ **Date:** _____

Directions: Draw an animal cell in the box. Label as many parts as you can. You can use your book and our class worksheets. Identify each part by coloring it the color indicated in the word box.

cell membrane (yellow)	nucleolus (blue)	lysosome (green)	cytoplasm (light green)
mitochondria (orange)	nucleus (red)	ribosome (black)	vacuole (brown)

Animal Cell

Comparing Plant and Animal Cells—Assessment

Directions: Complete the chart below; then answer the questions.

Cell Part or Organelle	Is It Found in a Plant Cell?	Is It Found in an Animal Cell?
Cell Membrane		
Cell Wall		
Chloroplast		
Cytoplasm		
Endoplasmic reticulum		
Lysosome		
Mitochondria		
Nucleus		
Nucleolus		
Ribosome		
Vacuole		

Questions

1. What cell parts do animal cells have that plant cells do not have?

2. What cell parts do plant cells have that animal cells do not have?

3. Why do plant cells have cell walls and animal cells do not?

4. Why do you think plant cells have bigger vacuoles than animal cells?

Vocabulary List—Lesson 4

1. Microscope
2. Base
3. Body tube
4. Coarse focus adjustment
5. Diaphragm
6. Eyepiece
7. Fine focus adjustment
8. High-powered objective
9. Inclination joint
10. Low-powered objective
11. Light source

12. Revolving nosepiece
13. Stage
14. Stage clips
15. Next to
16. On top of
17. Near
18. Far
19. View
20. Raise
21. Lower
22. Arm

KWL Chart
Microscopes

Name: _____ **Date:** _____

K	W	L
What do I **K**now about microscopes?	What do I **W**ant to know about microscopes?	What have I **L**earned about microscopes?

Activity 1
Procedures for Using a
Compound Microscope

(Time: 1 minute 51 seconds)

Name: _____ **Date:** _____

You will watch a video clip about how to use a compound microscope. After watching the video, fill in the missing words.

When first adjusting the microscope for a new slide, always use the lowest power

objective and start with the nosepiece at its lowest setting. Then turn the coarse

adjustment _____ upward and move the objective away from the slide

_____ the specimen comes into focus.

　　Improve the focus using the fine adjustment knob. By starting at the

lowest _____and focusing upward, you will not have to worry about

_____ the slide by lowering the objective lens into it.

　　Once the _____ is focused, you can change directly to magnifications

without changing the focus. However, move the nosepiece _____ so that the

newly selected objective lens doesn't strike the _____. This could damage

the lens and the specimen. _____ viewing through the eyepiece, many

people keep both eyes _____to lessen eye strain.

Activity 2
Label the Microscope

Directions: Use the cut-out pieces in the bag to label the microscope.

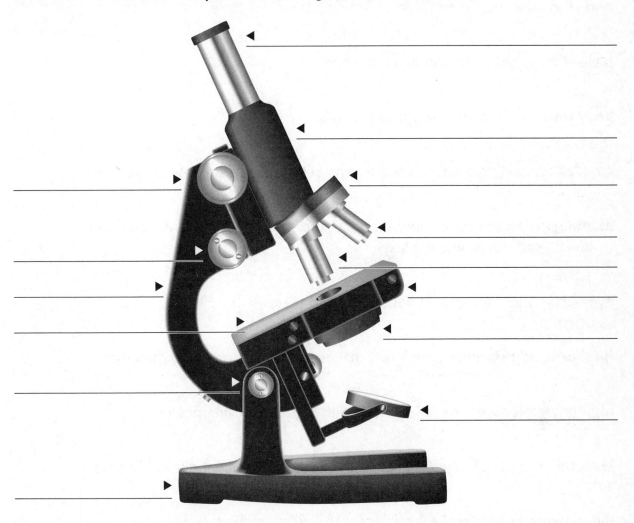

arm	light source	revolving nosepiece
stage	inclination joint	low-powered objective
eyepiece	fine focus adjustment	high-powered objective
coarse focus adjustment	diaphragm	body tube
base	stage clips	

Directions: Cut out the words above and use the Velcro backing to label the parts of the microscope on the posterboard.

✂

arm—this attaches the eyepiece and body tube to the base

base—this supports the whole microscope

body tube—the tube that supports the eyepiece

coarse focus adjustment—a knob that makes large adjustments to the focus

diaphragm—an adjustable opening under the stage where different amounts of light can come onto the stage

eyepiece—where you place your eye

fine focus adjustment—a knob that makes small adjustments to the focus

high-powered objective—a large lens with high magnifying power

inclination joint—an adjustable knob that lets the arm tilt at different angles

low-powered objective—a small lens with low magnifying power

light source—this directs light upward onto the slide

revolving nosepiece—the rotating device that holds the lenses

stage—where a slide is placed

stage clips—metal clips that hold slides onto the stage

Vocabulary List—Lesson 5

Beds and Alarms

1. Bed
2. Alarm
3. Clock
4. Bell
5. Whistle
6. Radio
7. Mattress
8. Pillow
9. Sounds
10. Sheets
11. Blankets
12. Pillow
13. Headboard
14. Footboard
15. Invention

Literary Elements

1. Characters
2. Plot
3. Setting
4. Point of view

Literary Genres

1. Picture books
2. Easy to read
3. Fantasy
4. Historical fiction
5. Mystery
6. Realistic fiction
7. Nonfiction books
8. Folktales
9. Poetry

When Listening to
"Do You Believe in Magic?"

1. What images did you imagine?

2. How did the song make you feel?

3. Describe the sounds you heard in the song.

Activity 1
The Magic Bed

Directions: With your copy of *The Magic Bed,* answer the following questions:

Teacher reads the title of the story and asks students…

    1. What do you think this story is about?

    2. Why do you think that?

Students read aloud to the first stopping point (2–3 pages). Teacher asks students…

    3. What is the story about?

    4. What do you think will happen next?

Students read with a partner to the next stopping point (2–4 pages). Teacher asks students…

    5. What has happened?

    6. How did your predictions turn out?

    7. What do you think will happen now?

Students read silently to the end of the story. Teacher asks students…

    8. How did the story end?

    9. How did your predictions turn out?

The Magic Bed
T-Chart

Name: _____   **Date:** _____

Directions: Complete the chart with a partner.

The **good** things about the bed in the story	The **not so good** things about the bed in the story
+	**–**

Assessment of a Mini Presentation

	Student A	Student B	Student C	Student D	Student E
As a Presenter					
Mentions materials to be used in constructing the bed					
Mentions devices					
Explains devices					
Mentions personal experience					
Works to form complete and grammatically correct sentences					
Additional notes					
As a Listener					
Shows active listening					
Asks relevant questions					
Shows respect for the speaker					
Works to form complete grammatically correct statements or questions					
Additional notes					

Vocabulary List—Unit Lesson 6

1. Inch

2. Foot/feet

3. Yard

4. Ruler

5. Yardstick

6. Word problem

7. Broken ruler

8. Metric ruler

9. Linear measurement

10. Estimate

11. Equivalent

12. Meter stick

13. Brainstorm

14. Length

15. Height

16. Width

17. Calculate

18. Actual distance

19. Required distance

20. Minimum

21. Maximum

22. Rectangle

23. Perimeter

24. Data

25. Inside

26. Outside

27. Tape measure

28. Clipboard

29. Graph paper

30. Centimeter

31. Customary

Day 1 Activity
Frayer Model

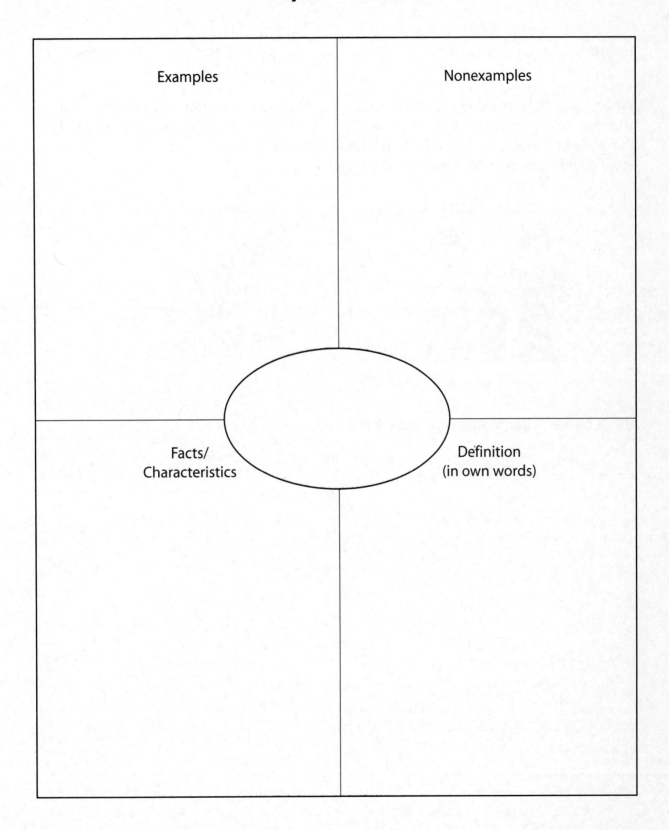

Examples

Nonexamples

Facts/
Characteristics

Definition
(in own words)

Day 2 Activity
Broken Rulers

Name: _____ **Date:** _____

When I was little, my dad wanted to make a dollhouse for my dolls. We had to measure the height of the dolls to make sure we made a big enough dollhouse. The only thing we had was a broken ruler that started at three inches.
How could I measure the height of my dolls?

Use a broken ruler to measure these lines.

_____

_____ inches

_____

_____ inches

_____

_____ inches

Assessment Rubric

Achievement	Understanding of Problem	Strategies	Accuracy
4 Outstanding	Identifies the question and the components of the problem accurately	Uses various strategies correctly: ___ makes a list ___ makes a table ___ draws a picture ___ finds a pattern ___ works backward ___ guesses and checks ___ uses base-10 blocks or other manipulatives ___ other: _____	Arrives at correct answer Correctly labels answer
3 Advanced	Identifies the question but ignores one component	Uses strategies incompletely for the problem or for getting the correct solution	Correct answer with incorrect labels or correct labels with minor calculation error
2 Basic	Identifies the question but ignores more than one component of the problem	Uses inappropriate strategies for the type of problem or reaches a subgoal and does not finish	One or more subcomponents correct but wrong answer overall Based on incorrect plan or no evident plan, without correct labels
1 Minimal	Does not identify the question and ignores more than one component of the problem	Inappropriate strategy started No attempt to try alternative strategy Numbers simply recopied Subgoals not reached Problem not finished	Wrong answer without correct subcomponents or labels or no answer given

Day 2 Activity
Personal Reference

Name: _____   Date: _____

Personal Reference Sheet

Find items that measure about the following lengths.

Write down the name of the item and its actual length.

Don't forget to include the unit (centimeters, inches, or feet).

	Item	**Actual length**
Metric		
1 cm.	*Ones cube*	*1 cm.*
	_____	_____
	_____	_____
10 cm.	_____	_____
	_____	_____
U.S. Customary		
1 in.	_____	_____
	_____	_____
1 ft.	_____	_____
	_____	_____

Day 3 Activity
Measure Height

Hunt for Large Objects

Name: _____ **Date:** _____

Find large items to measure with your U.S. customary ruler or yardstick. Draw a picture and list the height or width of at least three large objects. For example, you can measure the width of the blackboard. Don't forget to include the unit (inches, feet, or yards).

Object	Picture	Measurement
Blackboard		Height: 42 inches

_____

_____

_____

Day 3 Activity
Word Problems

Name: _____ **Date:** _____ **Time:** _____

Length Word Problems

Show your thinking.

1. Luisa needs 10 feet of cloth to make a skirt. She went to the fabric store and found out that they only sell the cloth she needs by the yard. How many yards does she need to buy?

2. Rafael is 43 inches tall. The beach towel he used was 2 yards long. Which was longer, Rafael or his towel? How much longer?

3. Create your own length problem.

Day 4 Activity
Citation (1)

(Same height as door)

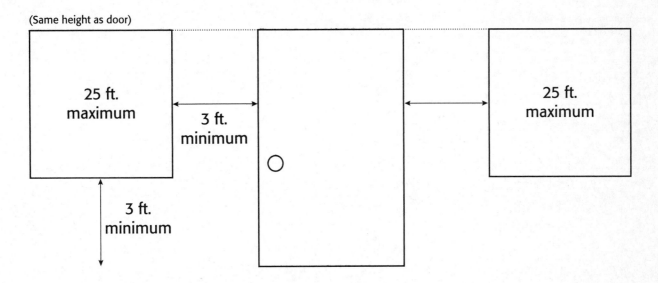

25 ft. maximum

3 ft. minimum

3 ft. minimum

25 ft. maximum

Citation

We have measured your display and found that you are in violation of the following:

_____ 3 feet minimum space to door
Your poster is _____ from the door.
You should move it _____.

_____ 3 feet minimum space from floor
Your poster is _____ from the floor.
You should move it _____.

_____ 25 feet maximum length of poster
Your poster is _____ long.
You need to make it _____ shorter.

_____ same height as door
Your poster is _____ taller than the door.
You need to move it _____.

Thank you,
Your friendly 4th-grade measurement team

Day 4 Activity
Citation (2)

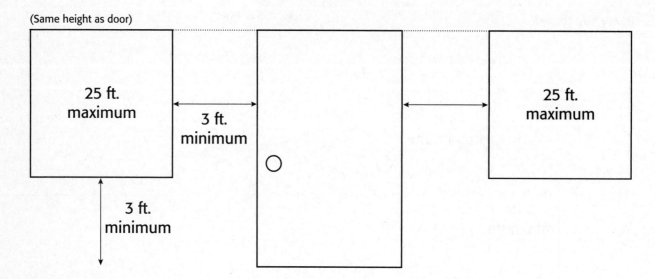

(Same height as door)

25 ft. maximum

3 ft. minimum

3 ft. minimum

25 ft. maximum

Citation

We have measured your display and found that you are in violation of the following:

_____ 3 feet minimum space to door
Your poster is _____ from the door.
You should move it _____.

_____ 3 feet minimum space from floor
Your poster is _____ from the floor.
You should move it _____.

Thank you,
Your friendly 4th-grade measurement team

Vocabulary List—Unit Lesson 7

1. Brainstorm
2. Graphic organizer
3. Feedback
4. Author
5. Illustrator
6. Elaborate
7. Collaboration
8. Revision
9. Editing

10. Strategy
11. Capital letters
12. Punctuation
13. Sentences
14. Edit
15. Save
16. Delete
17. Clip art

Writers' Workshop T-Chart

Problem	Solution

What Do Good Writers Do?

✓ Use a prewriting strategy

✓ Use the teacher models for help

✓ Sound out words to help spell

✓ Check for capital letters

✓ Check for punctuation

✓ Check for complete sentences

✓ Reread before turning it in

KWL
What I Know about
How a Book Is Made

This is what I <u>K</u>now about how a book is made.

_____

_____

_____

_____

This is what I <u>W</u>ant to know about how a book is made.

_____

_____

_____

_____

This is what I <u>L</u>earned about how a book is made.

_____

_____

_____

_____

Index